Climate Change and Natural Capital: Supporting Ecosystem Services, Biodiversity, Carbon Sequestration, Sustainable Development, and Green Infrastructure

Copyright

Climate Change and Natural Capital: Supporting Ecosystem Services, Biodiversity, Carbon Sequestration, Sustainable Development, and Green Infrastructure

© 2025 Robert C. Brears

ISBN (eBook): 978-1-991368-33-1

ISBN (Paperback): 978-1-991368-34-8

Published by Global Climate Solutions

First Edition, 2025

Cover design and interior layout by Global Climate Solutions

Table of Contents

Introduction

Natural capital refers to the stock of natural resources—such as air, water, soil, forests, oceans, and biodiversity—that generate goods and services vital to human survival and prosperity. It provides the foundation upon which societies and economies depend, from clean drinking water and fertile soil to pollination, carbon storage, and climate regulation. Unlike produced or financial capital, natural capital is finite and often irreplaceable. As pressures on ecosystems intensify, the concept has become essential for rethinking how humanity measures wealth and progress. Recognizing natural systems as assets with measurable value reframes them not as externalities but as integral to the functioning of modern economies.

The 21st century presents formidable challenges that highlight the fragility of natural capital. Rapid population growth, accelerating urbanization, resource overextraction, and the intensifying effects of climate change are eroding ecosystems at unprecedented rates. Forests shrink, fisheries collapse, and biodiversity declines, while greenhouse gas emissions destabilize the global climate. These disruptions reveal the risks of undervaluing nature: economic volatility, heightened disaster vulnerability, and reduced quality of life. By failing to account for environmental costs and benefits, decision-making in both public and private sectors often ignores the depletion of natural assets. This oversight threatens not only ecological sustainability but also long-term economic resilience and social stability.

The concept of natural capital offers a pathway toward more comprehensive accounting of environmental contributions. By assessing ecosystems as capital stocks that yield flows of services, it is possible to better understand trade-offs, identify sustainable limits, and incorporate ecological realities into planning. Methods for valuing natural capital—ranging from market-based approaches to non-market assessments—have expanded significantly in recent decades, shaping frameworks for environmental policy and corporate strategy. Governments, businesses, and communities are increasingly exploring tools that integrate natural capital into decision-making, from accounting systems and indices to investment practices and governance mechanisms.

This book examines the foundations, frameworks, and future of natural capital in detail. It explores its conceptual origins, measurement tools, and the governance structures that enable implementation. It highlights how financial markets, business practices, and investment strategies are evolving to incorporate natural capital considerations. It examines the critical role of terrestrial, freshwater, marine, and urban ecosystems in sustaining natural capital. It also considers how the concept intersects with global climate mitigation and adaptation strategies, underscoring its role in responding to the defining challenge of this century. Finally, it looks forward to future directions, including digital tools, cross-sectoral integration, and emerging approaches that will shape how natural capital evolves as both a scientific framework and a policy tool.

The aim of this book is to provide a structured, comprehensive understanding of natural capital, bridging ecological knowledge with economic, financial, and policy perspectives. By examining its multiple dimensions and applications, it seeks to equip policymakers, professionals, researchers, and students with a framework for engaging with one of the most important concepts of sustainability.

Chapter 1: Defining Natural Capital

Natural capital refers to the world's stock of natural assets—including soil, air, water, and living organisms—that provide essential goods and services underpinning human life and economic activity. Unlike manufactured or financial capital, natural capital is not created by humans, yet it forms the foundation upon which societies and economies depend. Clean water supplies, fertile soils, pollination, carbon storage, and flood regulation are just a few of the benefits derived from these ecological assets. Understanding natural capital requires framing ecosystems not simply as background environments but as critical, productive systems whose preservation is vital for resilience and sustainability.

Origins and Evolution of the Concept

The idea of natural capital has its intellectual roots in both economics and ecology, reflecting a long-standing effort to connect the value of natural systems with human well-being. Early economic thought in the 18th and 19th centuries often recognized land and natural resources as essential factors of production alongside labor and capital. Thinkers such as Adam Smith and David Ricardo considered land to be a critical input to economic activity, while Thomas Malthus highlighted the limits of natural resources in supporting population growth. However, as industrialization advanced, mainstream economic theory increasingly focused on manufactured and financial capital, with nature relegated to the role of a backdrop or assumed to be abundant and resilient.

During the 20th century, particularly in the decades following World War II, the rapid expansion of economies around the world created new pressures on ecosystems. Industrial growth, agricultural intensification, and urbanization led to widespread environmental degradation. The emergence of ecology as a scientific discipline provided a clearer understanding of the interdependence between ecosystems and human activity. Ecologists described the flow of energy, nutrients, and services within natural systems, laying the foundation for linking ecological processes to economic value. By the 1960s and 1970s, rising awareness of pollution, resource scarcity, and biodiversity loss spurred debates on whether economic growth could be sustained without accounting for environmental limits.

The term "natural capital" began to gain prominence in the 1970s and 1980s, as environmental economists sought to frame ecosystems in the language of capital assets familiar to policymakers and businesses. Herman Daly and Robert Costanza were among those who advanced the concept, arguing that natural resources and ecosystem functions should be treated as forms of capital comparable to machinery or infrastructure. By doing so, they emphasized that ecosystems produce flows of benefits over time and that their degradation represents a depreciation of wealth. This reframing allowed environmental concerns to be articulated in economic terms, making them more accessible to decision-makers in governments and corporations.

The evolution of natural capital was also influenced by the broader sustainability movement, particularly following the publication of the Brundtland Report in 1987. The report defined sustainable development as meeting present needs without compromising the ability of future generations to meet their own, an idea that aligns closely with preserving natural capital stocks. During the 1990s, the integration of natural capital into global discussions on sustainable development gained momentum, supported by international institutions, non-governmental organizations, and academic research. Concepts such as "ecological footprint" and "ecosystem services" became widely used tools to measure and communicate the impact of human activities on natural systems.

By the early 21st century, natural capital had become central to efforts to reform national accounting systems. Traditional measures of economic performance, such as gross domestic product, failed to capture the depletion of natural assets. Initiatives like the United Nations' System of Environmental-Economic Accounting (SEEA) and the World Bank's Wealth Accounting and the Valuation of

Ecosystem Services (WAVES) program sought to integrate natural capital into economic statistics, providing governments with more accurate pictures of their long-term wealth. At the same time, the rise of corporate sustainability reporting encouraged businesses to assess their dependence on and impact upon natural capital, linking ecological considerations with risk management and long-term profitability.

The evolution of the natural capital concept reflects a gradual but profound shift in the way societies view the relationship between nature and the economy. What was once considered external or inexhaustible is now understood as scarce, valuable, and in need of careful stewardship. The recognition that natural systems provide indispensable services, from climate regulation to soil fertility, has reframed environmental protection as an investment rather than a cost. This perspective has been essential in shaping policy, guiding scientific inquiry, and informing financial innovation, ensuring that natural capital continues to evolve as a central framework for addressing sustainability challenges.

Components of Natural Capital

Natural capital can be understood as the stock of natural assets that provide goods and services essential to human societies. These assets encompass a wide array of systems, each with unique functions and contributions to ecological stability and economic prosperity. To analyze natural capital effectively, it is often divided into key components: renewable resources, non-renewable resources, ecosystems and biodiversity, and the regulatory and cultural services derived from nature. Each component plays a distinct role, and together they form the foundation of natural wealth upon which human well-being depends.

One of the most visible components of natural capital is renewable resources. These are assets that can regenerate and replenish if managed sustainably, such as forests, freshwater systems, soils, and fish stocks. Forests, for example, provide timber and fuelwood while also delivering critical ecosystem services like carbon sequestration, water regulation, and habitat for biodiversity. Freshwater systems supply drinking water, irrigation, and energy through hydropower. Soils provide the basis for agriculture, storing nutrients and supporting food production. Fish stocks offer a renewable source of protein for billions of people worldwide. However, renewable resources are only sustainable within ecological limits. Overexploitation can lead to depletion, with forests becoming degraded, soils eroding, or fisheries collapsing if extraction exceeds natural regeneration rates. As a result, managing renewable resources requires balancing current consumption with long-term capacity.

Non-renewable resources form another major category of natural capital. These include fossil fuels, minerals, and metals that cannot regenerate on human time scales. Coal, oil, and natural gas have historically powered industrial development, while minerals like copper, iron, and rare earth elements underpin modern technology and infrastructure. Although these resources provide immense value, their extraction often results in environmental degradation, habitat destruction, and pollution. Moreover, reliance on non-renewables raises questions of intergenerational equity, as their finite nature means future generations may be deprived of their benefits. Recognizing non-renewables as part of natural capital underscores the importance of strategies such as efficiency improvements, recycling, and a transition toward renewable energy to reduce pressures on finite stocks.

Beyond tangible resources, ecosystems and biodiversity constitute critical components of natural capital. Ecosystems are complex networks of organisms interacting with each other and with their environment. They provide regulating, supporting, provisioning, and cultural services. For example, wetlands filter pollutants and reduce flood risks, forests regulate local and global climates, and coral reefs protect coastlines from storm surges. Biodiversity underpins the resilience of ecosystems by enabling them to adapt to changes and disturbances. Genetic diversity in crops, for instance, provides the basis for developing varieties that can withstand pests, diseases, or climate stress. Without healthy biodiversity, ecosystems lose functionality, compromising the services they deliver. The recognition of biodiversity as a cornerstone of natural capital emphasizes that species and habitats are not just valuable for their intrinsic worth but also for the critical roles they play in sustaining human life.

Another essential element of natural capital lies in its regulatory and cultural functions. Regulatory services include processes such as carbon storage, air purification, nutrient cycling, and water regulation, which maintain environmental stability. These services often go unnoticed until they are degraded, at which point their absence becomes costly. For instance, the loss of wetlands can lead to increased flood damage and higher expenditures on engineered flood defenses. Cultural services represent the non-material benefits derived from nature, including recreation, spiritual enrichment, aesthetic appreciation, and cultural identity. Landscapes, rivers, and forests often hold deep significance for communities, shaping traditions, values, and well-being in ways that extend beyond material wealth.

Together, renewable and non-renewable resources, ecosystems, biodiversity, and regulatory and cultural services form a holistic picture of natural capital. Each component interacts with and supports the others, creating interdependencies that sustain both ecological and economic systems. The depletion of one element—such as biodiversity—can ripple through the entire system, undermining resource availability, regulatory functions, and cultural connections. By recognizing and understanding the components of natural capital, societies can design more informed strategies for conservation, sustainable use, and integration into economic frameworks. This comprehensive view ensures that natural capital is not treated as a collection of isolated resources but as a dynamic system essential to the long-term viability of human life and prosperity.

Natural Capital Versus Ecosystem Services

The concepts of natural capital and ecosystem services are closely linked, yet they serve different roles in understanding the relationship between human societies and the environment. Natural capital refers to the stock of natural resources—such as forests, wetlands, soils, and oceans—that function as assets capable of generating value. Ecosystem services, on the other hand, represent the flows of benefits that people receive from these stocks. In other words, natural capital can be seen as the underlying assets, while ecosystem services are the returns produced by those assets. This distinction is fundamental for both theoretical clarity and practical applications in policy, business, and environmental management.

Natural capital emphasizes the idea of nature as a form of wealth. Just as financial capital generates interest and manufactured capital produces goods, natural capital provides renewable flows of ecosystem services. Forests, for instance, represent a stock of natural capital, while the timber, climate regulation, and recreational opportunities they provide are ecosystem services. By framing ecosystems in terms of capital assets, natural capital creates a framework for analyzing trade-offs, depreciation, and investment in ways familiar to economists and policymakers. This framing encourages a long-term perspective: sustaining natural capital stocks is essential if societies are to secure continuous flows of benefits over time.

Ecosystem services complement this by focusing attention on the direct and indirect benefits nature provides to people. These benefits are often categorized into provisioning, regulating, cultural, and supporting services. Provisioning services include tangible goods such as food, water, and raw materials. Regulating services encompass processes like flood control, carbon sequestration, and air purification. Cultural services refer to non-material benefits such as recreation, aesthetic enjoyment, and spiritual significance. Supporting services, like nutrient cycling and soil formation, underlie all other categories. By articulating these benefits in human-centered terms, ecosystem services make the value of nature visible in everyday life, highlighting the practical and immediate importance of healthy ecosystems.

The distinction between natural capital and ecosystem services also has implications for measurement and management. Natural capital accounting focuses on quantifying the stocks of assets and tracking their changes over time, much like financial balance sheets. This includes estimating the size, condition, and sustainability of forests, wetlands, or fisheries. Ecosystem services assessments, by contrast, often measure flows of benefits, evaluating how much clean water a watershed provides, how much carbon a forest absorbs, or how much recreation a park enables. Both approaches are complementary: without healthy natural capital, the flows of ecosystem services decline, and without recognition of ecosystem services, the value of natural capital remains invisible in decision-making.

This relationship also affects policy frameworks. When governments develop strategies for conservation or sustainable use, they often combine natural capital assessments with ecosystem services valuation. Protecting a wetland, for example, safeguards a stock of natural capital while ensuring the continued flow of regulating services like flood protection and water filtration. The integration of both concepts enables more comprehensive approaches to environmental governance, making the case for investment in conservation not just on ethical grounds but also in terms of tangible economic and social benefits.

Businesses likewise use both frameworks to assess risks and opportunities. Natural capital thinking helps companies recognize their dependencies on natural assets and the long-term sustainability of their operations. Ecosystem services assessments allow them to identify specific benefits or vulnerabilities, such as water availability, pollination for agriculture, or exposure to climate risks. Together, they inform corporate strategies, investment decisions, and sustainability reporting, ensuring that the links between ecological systems and economic activity are explicitly acknowledged.

While closely related, natural capital and ecosystem services are not interchangeable. Treating them as synonyms risks obscuring their complementary roles. Natural capital highlights the stocks, reminding decision-makers of the need to maintain and replenish ecological assets. Ecosystem services highlight the flows, emphasizing the day-to-day benefits people receive and the costs of their loss. Understanding both dimensions is crucial for creating policies and practices that balance conservation, development, and long-term resilience.

Ethical and Philosophical Dimensions

The concept of natural capital raises important ethical and philosophical questions about how societies view, value, and relate to the natural world. While the framework provides a practical means to incorporate ecological considerations into economic and policy decisions, it also risks reducing nature to a commodity measured primarily in monetary terms. This tension reflects deeper debates about human responsibility toward the environment, the intrinsic versus instrumental value of nature, and intergenerational justice. Exploring these dimensions is essential for understanding both the strengths and the limitations of natural capital as a guiding concept.

At the core of the ethical debate lies the question of value. Natural capital emphasizes the benefits ecosystems provide to humans, framing them as assets that generate flows of goods and services. This anthropocentric approach aligns with economic and policy systems that prioritize measurable outcomes, but it can obscure the intrinsic value of nature—its worth independent of human use. Many philosophers and ethicists argue that species, ecosystems, and landscapes possess inherent value that deserves respect and protection regardless of their utility to people. For example, a rare species may have little immediate economic importance but still hold moral significance as part of Earth's shared heritage. The tension between intrinsic and instrumental values highlights the risk of reducing natural systems to mere components of human wealth.

Another ethical dimension concerns commodification. Assigning financial value to ecosystems through the language of natural capital can promote conservation by demonstrating the economic

14

importance of protecting natural assets. However, critics warn that this approach may reinforce a worldview in which nature is valued only when it can be monetized. For instance, a wetland may be protected because of its role in water filtration and carbon storage, but not for its cultural or spiritual significance. This instrumental framing risks marginalizing values that cannot be easily quantified and could create markets that prioritize short-term profits over long-term ecological integrity. The ethical challenge lies in finding a balance between demonstrating economic relevance and maintaining recognition of non-monetary values.

The philosophical dimension also extends to justice and fairness. Natural capital frameworks raise questions about how benefits and burdens are distributed across societies. Ecosystem services are not shared equally; some communities rely heavily on local natural capital for subsistence, while others benefit indirectly through global systems of trade and environmental regulation. For example, indigenous communities may depend directly on forests and rivers for livelihoods, while urban populations benefit from carbon sequestration performed by distant ecosystems. Ethical considerations demand that natural capital management respect the rights and knowledge of local and indigenous peoples, ensuring they have a voice in decisions that affect their resources. Without such safeguards, natural capital policies could perpetuate inequities by privileging the interests of wealthier or more powerful groups.

Intergenerational justice is another key concern. The framing of natural capital emphasizes the importance of maintaining stocks so that future generations can enjoy the benefits of ecosystem services. This raises questions about the responsibilities of current generations to preserve natural assets and avoid passing on ecological debts. Philosophers argue that sustainability requires acknowledging the rights of future people, who cannot participate in today's decision-making but will bear the consequences of resource depletion and environmental degradation. Natural capital accounting and investment strategies can support this ethical responsibility by highlighting long-term impacts, but only if they move beyond short-term economic calculations to embrace broader principles of stewardship and care.

A further philosophical question arises from the relationship between humans and nature. The natural capital framework often portrays ecosystems as external assets that provide inputs into human systems. This perspective can reinforce the notion of separation between people and the environment, rather than recognizing humans as embedded within ecological systems. Alternative philosophical traditions, including indigenous worldviews, emphasize interconnectedness, reciprocity, and the duty of care toward non-human life. Incorporating such perspectives into natural capital thinking can enrich the concept, grounding it in values that transcend economic utility and highlight the moral dimensions of environmental stewardship.

Finally, there is the issue of decision-making under uncertainty. Ecosystems are complex, dynamic, and not fully understood. Assigning values to natural capital often involves assumptions and approximations that may not capture the full scope of ecological processes. From an ethical standpoint, this uncertainty suggests a precautionary approach: when in doubt, societies should act to protect natural systems rather than risk irreversible harm. This principle aligns with the moral responsibility to safeguard natural capital not only for current benefits but also for future possibilities that may not yet be recognized or measurable.

In summary, the ethical and philosophical dimensions of natural capital challenge societies to consider more than economic efficiency. They invite reflection on intrinsic value, the risks of commodification, the distribution of benefits and burdens, intergenerational justice, cultural perspectives, and the moral obligations arising from ecological uncertainty. Addressing these issues ensures that natural capital is not simply a tool for economic integration but a framework that reflects humanity's broader responsibilities to the planet and to each other.

Chapter 2: Frameworks and Measurement

Frameworks and measurement approaches provide the foundation for understanding, quantifying, and integrating natural capital into decision-making. Without consistent methods and tools, the value of ecosystems remains invisible in economic, financial, and policy systems, leaving critical services undervalued or ignored. Establishing robust frameworks ensures comparability across contexts, while measurement systems translate ecological functions into tangible indicators and metrics.

This chapter examines the leading conceptual frameworks that guide the study and application of natural capital, from global initiatives to national and corporate systems. It also explores methods of measurement, including valuation approaches, accounting structures, and monitoring indicators that support evidence-based governance and investment. Through these lenses, natural capital becomes not only a scientific concept but also a practical tool for aligning environmental integrity with economic and social goals.

Valuation Methods

Valuation methods are central to the concept of natural capital because they provide ways of assigning measurable value to the goods and services ecosystems deliver. Without valuation, natural systems risk being overlooked in economic decision-making, as their contributions remain invisible on balance sheets or national accounts. Different approaches to valuation reflect both economic theory and ecological science, offering tools for assessing benefits ranging from food and timber to flood protection and cultural experiences. These methods can be broadly divided into market-based approaches, revealed preference methods, stated preference methods, and cost-based approaches.

Market-based approaches assign value to natural capital using observable prices in existing markets. For example, timber harvested from a forest, fish caught from the sea, or water supplied from a river can all be priced directly. This method works best when goods and services are traded openly and consistently, as markets provide clear signals of supply, demand, and scarcity. However, many ecosystem services—such as climate regulation or water filtration—are not traded in markets. As a result, market-based approaches capture only a subset of the value provided by natural capital and risk underestimating its broader importance.

Revealed preference methods attempt to uncover the value of ecosystem services by analyzing human behavior in related markets. A well-known example is the travel cost method, which estimates the recreational value of natural sites such as parks or beaches by observing how much people spend to visit them, including travel expenses, time, and entry fees. Another example is the hedonic pricing method, which infers the value of environmental amenities from differences in property prices. Homes near green spaces, lakes, or with cleaner air often sell for higher prices, reflecting the value people place on these services. These approaches provide indirect estimates of value but are limited to contexts where human behavior clearly reflects environmental preferences.

Stated preference methods are survey-based techniques designed to capture values that may not be revealed in market transactions. Contingent valuation is a common example, in which individuals are asked how much they would be willing to pay to preserve an ecosystem service or to accept compensation for its loss. Choice experiments extend this by presenting respondents with sets of hypothetical scenarios that vary in attributes and costs, allowing researchers to infer preferences across multiple dimensions. Stated preference methods are especially useful for valuing non-market benefits such as biodiversity, cultural services, or existence values—the worth people place on knowing that a species or ecosystem continues to exist, even if they never directly experience it. However, the reliability of survey-based methods can be challenged by biases in responses, such as overstatement or hypothetical behavior.

Cost-based approaches estimate the value of ecosystem services by examining the costs society would incur if they were lost or had to be replaced by human-made alternatives. For example, the value of wetlands can be inferred from the cost of building engineered flood protection if those wetlands were degraded. Similarly, the value of pollination by insects can be measured by the cost of replacing it with manual pollination. Avoided cost methods calculate the damages that ecosystems help prevent, such as reduced healthcare costs from cleaner air or savings from reduced disaster risk. While these approaches do not measure willingness to pay directly, they provide practical estimates that highlight the economic significance of natural systems.

Each valuation method has strengths and weaknesses, and in practice, a combination is often used to capture the full range of ecosystem benefits. Market-based approaches provide concrete numbers where markets exist, but they miss many non-market services. Revealed and stated preference methods fill these gaps, though they require careful design and interpretation. Cost-based approaches, meanwhile, emphasize the substitutability of natural systems with human-made alternatives, which may underestimate the irreplaceable qualities of ecosystems. Together, these methods contribute to a more complete understanding of natural capital, enabling decision-makers to integrate ecological considerations into economic planning, corporate strategies, and public policy.

Natural Capital Accounting Systems

Natural capital accounting systems provide structured frameworks for measuring, organizing, and integrating information about natural assets into economic and policy decision-making. Their purpose is to ensure that the contributions of ecosystems and resources are visible in national accounts, corporate reports, and financial planning. By systematically tracking stocks of natural capital and the flows of ecosystem services, these systems help identify trends in resource use, assess sustainability, and highlight the long-term costs of environmental degradation. They serve as essential tools for aligning economic development with ecological realities.

One of the most significant developments in this field is the United Nations' SEEA. The SEEA extends traditional national accounts by incorporating environmental information into economic statistics. It enables governments to track changes in ecosystems, resource use, and pollution alongside economic output, providing a fuller picture of national wealth. The SEEA includes two major components: the Central Framework, which covers stocks and flows of natural resources like water, energy, and timber, and the Ecosystem Accounting module, which focuses on the condition and services of ecosystems. Together, they allow policymakers to see how economic activity affects natural capital and how environmental change feeds back into economic performance.

In addition to global initiatives like the SEEA, natural capital accounting has been advanced by organizations such as the World Bank through its WAVES program. WAVES promotes the integration of natural capital into development planning by supporting countries in building their own accounting systems. By creating consistent measures of natural wealth, countries can track the sustainability of growth, identify environmental risks, and design policies that better balance economic development with conservation. For example, accounts on water use can inform decisions about irrigation efficiency, while forest accounts can reveal the costs of deforestation on both timber production and ecosystem services.

At the corporate level, natural capital accounting systems provide businesses with tools to measure their dependencies on and impacts upon ecosystems. Frameworks such as the Natural Capital Protocol guide companies in identifying, quantifying, and integrating natural capital into decision-making processes. These systems help firms assess risks—such as water scarcity that could disrupt supply chains—or opportunities, such as investments in ecosystem restoration that yield reputational and financial benefits. By incorporating natural capital into financial reports and risk assessments, companies can improve transparency, accountability, and long-term resilience. Investors, in turn, benefit from clearer insights into the environmental performance and sustainability of the firms they support.

Natural capital accounting systems also rely on advances in data collection, modeling, and technology. Remote sensing, satellite imagery, and geographic information systems (GIS) enable detailed tracking of land cover, deforestation, and ecosystem health. Advances in environmental indicators provide standardized ways of measuring ecosystem condition, biodiversity, and service flows. These technologies make it possible to generate consistent and comparable accounts across regions and time periods, reducing uncertainty and increasing the reliability of natural capital integration into planning. However, challenges remain in harmonizing data sources, ensuring accuracy, and addressing gaps in knowledge about ecosystem dynamics.

Despite these advances, natural capital accounting systems face limitations. Assigning precise values to ecosystems can be complex, as many services are intangible or occur on long time scales. Some critics argue that accounting systems risk oversimplifying ecological processes or reinforcing the commodification of nature. Others note that political and institutional challenges often hinder adoption, as integrating natural capital into decision-making can reveal trade-offs that are politically sensitive. For instance, recognizing the depletion of groundwater in accounts may force difficult choices between agricultural expansion and long-term sustainability. Addressing these challenges requires building capacity, fostering institutional commitment, and ensuring that accounting systems are not only technically sound but also socially and politically feasible.

Overall, natural capital accounting systems represent a major step toward embedding ecological considerations into economic governance. By treating ecosystems and resources as measurable assets, they provide decision-makers with the information needed to balance short-term growth with long-term sustainability. While technical and political hurdles remain, these systems continue to evolve, supported by international collaboration, technological innovation, and growing recognition of the vital role that natural capital plays in sustaining human prosperity.

Indicators and Metrics for Monitoring

Indicators and metrics are vital tools for monitoring the condition of natural capital and the services it provides. They transform complex ecological data into measurable variables that can be tracked over time, helping policymakers, businesses, and communities assess sustainability and detect early warning signs of degradation. Without clear indicators, the value of natural capital remains abstract, making it difficult to integrate into economic planning, corporate strategies, or governance frameworks. Effective indicators provide transparency, comparability, and accountability, enabling informed decisions at both local and global levels.

One important category of indicators focuses on the extent and condition of ecosystems. These include measures of land cover, forest area, wetland extent, coral reef health, or soil fertility. For example, the rate of deforestation can serve as a key indicator of forest natural capital, while soil organic carbon levels measure soil health and fertility. Condition indicators assess not just quantity but also quality, such as water clarity in lakes or species composition in grasslands. By tracking both extent and condition, decision-makers gain insights into whether ecosystems are being maintained, enhanced, or degraded over time.

A second category relates to resource flows and use, capturing how societies consume or depend on natural capital. These metrics include water withdrawal rates, fishery catches, timber harvests, and mineral extraction levels. Comparing these flows with natural regeneration or replenishment rates provides insights into sustainability. For instance, a fish stock harvested at levels above its reproductive capacity indicates overexploitation and potential collapse. Similarly, monitoring freshwater withdrawals relative to renewable supply helps reveal water stress in river basins. These indicators link ecological dynamics to economic activity, highlighting where resource use may exceed safe limits.

A third set of indicators measures the provision of ecosystem services. Provisioning services can be monitored through agricultural yields, freshwater availability, or timber production. Regulating services require more complex indicators, such as carbon sequestration rates, flood risk reduction from wetlands, or air quality improvements from urban green spaces. Cultural services are more difficult to quantify but can be tracked through visitor numbers to parks, surveys of aesthetic value, or measures of cultural heritage linked to landscapes. These indicators translate ecosystem functions into tangible benefits, demonstrating the contributions of natural capital to human well-being.

In addition, biodiversity indicators are central to monitoring natural capital. Species richness, abundance, and population trends reflect the resilience and stability of ecosystems. Genetic diversity within species and the presence of keystone species provide further insights into ecological health. Global indices, such as the Living Planet Index, aggregate data on species populations to show overall trends in biodiversity. Biodiversity indicators are particularly important because they reveal the capacity of ecosystems to continue providing services under changing conditions, making them critical for long-term sustainability.

Another key area involves economic and policy-related indicators that integrate natural capital into decision-making frameworks. These include measures of ecosystem service valuation, natural capital accounts within national statistics, or corporate disclosure of natural resource dependencies. Economic indicators such as adjusted net savings or inclusive wealth incorporate natural capital depreciation alongside produced and human capital. These metrics help governments and businesses evaluate whether current growth paths are depleting or maintaining natural assets. Linking ecological indicators with financial and policy metrics bridges the gap between science and decision-making.

Developing effective indicators and metrics requires addressing challenges of scale, comparability, and data availability. Ecosystem processes often operate across spatial and temporal boundaries that do not align neatly with political or economic systems. Indicators must therefore be designed to capture local realities while being scalable to national or global levels. Data gaps remain a persistent challenge, particularly in developing countries or remote ecosystems where monitoring infrastructure is limited. Advances in remote sensing, satellite imagery, and digital technologies are helping fill these gaps, providing new opportunities for consistent and timely data collection.

Finally, indicators must be designed with usability in mind. Complex ecological metrics may be scientifically robust but difficult for policymakers or businesses to interpret and act upon. Effective systems translate technical information into accessible formats that inform decision-making while retaining scientific credibility. Participatory approaches that involve local communities in monitoring can also increase relevance and legitimacy, ensuring that indicators reflect diverse values and priorities. When carefully developed, indicators and metrics become powerful tools for safeguarding natural capital, linking ecological science to economic and social decision-making in ways that are transparent, measurable, and actionable.

Limitations and Critiques

While natural capital frameworks and accounting systems provide valuable tools for integrating ecological concerns into economic and policy decision-making, they are not without limitations and critiques. These approaches have generated considerable debate across disciplines, reflecting both technical challenges and deeper philosophical concerns about how nature is valued and represented. Understanding these critiques is essential for ensuring that natural capital approaches are applied thoughtfully and without overlooking their shortcomings.

A central limitation lies in the difficulty of measurement. Ecosystems are complex, dynamic, and interdependent, making it challenging to capture their full range of functions and services in quantitative terms. For instance, while carbon sequestration in forests may be measured with some precision, the cultural or spiritual significance of the same forest to local communities is far harder to quantify. This unevenness creates gaps in accounting systems, where certain values are recognized and others remain invisible. The reliance on quantification risks privileging what can be measured over what is most meaningful, leaving out critical dimensions of human–nature relationships.

Closely related to this issue is the problem of monetization. By framing ecosystems as capital assets, natural capital approaches often seek to assign financial value to the services nature provides. While this can make ecological benefits more visible to decision-makers, it also raises the risk of commodifying nature in ways that reduce its significance to purely economic terms. Assigning a dollar value to biodiversity, for example, may obscure its intrinsic worth and its role in maintaining ecological integrity beyond immediate human use. Critics argue that this framing reinforces an anthropocentric worldview, where nature is valued only for what it can provide to humans rather than for its own sake.

Another critique is the assumption of substitutability between natural capital and other forms of capital. In economic theory, capital is often interchangeable: losses in one type of capital can be offset by gains in another. However, many natural assets are irreplaceable or non-substitutable. For example, extinct species cannot be restored through financial investment, and lost wetlands cannot always be replaced by engineered infrastructure. Treating natural systems as substitutable risks encouraging trade-offs that undermine long-term ecological sustainability. It also creates a false sense of security that human-made solutions can always replace natural processes, which may not hold true under conditions of ecological collapse or irreversible change.

Equity and justice concerns also feature prominently in critiques of natural capital. Ecosystem services are not distributed equally, and the benefits of conservation or the costs of degradation often fall unevenly across societies. Indigenous peoples and local communities may rely heavily on natural capital for livelihoods and cultural identity, yet they are often excluded from decision-making processes that adopt natural capital frameworks. Efforts to create markets for ecosystem services can, in some cases, restrict community access to resources or impose external values that conflict with local traditions. This raises ethical questions about whose values are prioritized and who bears the burdens of conservation policies.

Natural capital approaches also face institutional and political challenges. Governments and businesses may adopt accounting frameworks without fully integrating them into decision-making, resulting in symbolic commitments rather than substantive change. Political pressures can limit the willingness to recognize ecological limits, especially when short-term economic growth goals conflict with long-term sustainability. Moreover, the complexity of natural capital accounts can make them difficult to communicate to non-specialists, reducing their practical impact on policy and public engagement. Without strong institutional frameworks, natural capital risks becoming a technocratic exercise with limited influence on real-world decisions.

Another limitation is uncertainty. Ecological systems are inherently variable and influenced by multiple interacting drivers, including climate change, land use, and pollution. Predicting future states of ecosystems is fraught with uncertainty, and valuation exercises often rely on assumptions that may not hold true in practice. For example, models estimating the economic value of carbon sequestration may underestimate or overestimate actual performance under changing climate conditions. This uncertainty complicates efforts to use natural capital metrics as definitive guides for decision-making, raising the risk of misinformed or misguided policies.

Finally, there is the critique that natural capital frameworks may reinforce existing economic paradigms rather than challenging them.

By embedding nature into the logic of capital and markets, these approaches may legitimize systems that contributed to ecological degradation in the first place. Some critics argue that rather than adapting nature to fit economic frameworks, societies should rethink economic models themselves to prioritize ecological integrity and human well-being. This perspective emphasizes that natural capital is a useful tool but not a substitute for deeper transformations in how societies conceive of growth, wealth, and sustainability.

In sum, natural capital approaches face technical, ethical, and political limitations. Challenges of measurement, monetization, and substitutability raise questions about their comprehensiveness and accuracy. Equity concerns highlight the risk of marginalizing local and indigenous perspectives. Institutional inertia and uncertainty complicate their practical application, while broader critiques point to the risk of reinforcing flawed economic paradigms. These limitations do not render natural capital frameworks useless, but they underscore the need for caution, inclusivity, and humility in their application, ensuring that they complement rather than dominate broader sustainability efforts.

Chapter 3: Policy and Governance Dimensions

The policy and governance dimensions of natural capital determine how ecosystems are valued, protected, and integrated into development strategies. While scientific frameworks highlight the importance of natural assets, effective governance translates these insights into laws, regulations, and institutional practices that guide resource use and management. International agreements set global priorities, national policies establish legal and economic frameworks, and local governance ensures implementation on the ground. Together, these layers of authority shape how societies balance ecological integrity with economic growth. Understanding governance is therefore essential for embedding natural capital within sustainable development pathways and ensuring equitable outcomes.

International Policy Frameworks

International policy frameworks play a central role in shaping how natural capital is recognized, managed, and integrated into global sustainability agendas. They provide shared principles, goals, and mechanisms that encourage countries to protect ecosystems, measure their contributions, and ensure that natural assets are sustained for future generations. These frameworks establish a common language for cooperation, enabling governments, organizations, and businesses to align their strategies with global objectives while addressing local priorities. Over the past few decades, multiple international agreements and initiatives have emerged that directly or indirectly address natural capital.

One of the most influential frameworks is the Convention on Biological Diversity (CBD), adopted in 1992 at the Earth Summit in Rio de Janeiro. The CBD recognizes biodiversity as a critical component of natural capital, emphasizing conservation, sustainable use, and equitable sharing of benefits. Its Aichi Biodiversity Targets, and more recently the Kunming-Montreal Global Biodiversity

Framework adopted in 2022, call on nations to halt biodiversity loss, protect ecosystems, and integrate natural capital considerations into development planning. By setting global goals, the CBD has provided a foundation for countries to embed natural capital into national strategies and biodiversity action plans, even though progress toward these targets has often been uneven.

The United Nations Framework Convention on Climate Change (UNFCCC) also intersects with natural capital, particularly through its focus on mitigation and adaptation. Ecosystems such as forests, wetlands, and oceans act as critical carbon sinks, making them central to global climate strategies. Mechanisms like REDD+ (Reducing Emissions from Deforestation and Forest Degradation) highlight the role of natural capital in achieving emission reductions while supporting sustainable development. The Paris Agreement of 2015 further strengthened this connection, recognizing the importance of maintaining ecosystems and biodiversity in addressing climate change. International climate policy has thus reinforced the value of natural capital by linking it directly to climate goals.

Sustainable development has been another major driver of natural capital integration. The 2030 Agenda for Sustainable Development and its 17 Sustainable Development Goals (SDGs) include explicit recognition of ecosystems, biodiversity, and natural resource management. Goals such as SDG 14 (Life Below Water) and SDG 15 (Life on Land) directly address the conservation and sustainable use of natural capital. Other goals, including those related to poverty, food security, and health, also depend on ecosystems and biodiversity. The SDGs promote a holistic approach, encouraging nations to integrate natural capital considerations across multiple sectors and levels of governance.

International financial institutions have supported these frameworks by developing tools and guidelines for integrating natural capital into decision-making. The World Bank's WAVES program assists countries in creating natural capital accounts, aligning with the United Nations' System of Environmental-Economic Accounting. These initiatives aim to embed natural capital into national economic planning and development strategies, ensuring that environmental sustainability is not treated separately from economic growth. By supporting capacity-building and data development, these institutions play a vital role in operationalizing international commitments.

Trade and environmental agreements also shape natural capital management. The Convention on International Trade in Endangered Species of Wild Fauna and Flora (CITES) regulates trade in species to prevent overexploitation, thereby safeguarding critical components of natural capital. Regional agreements, such as the European Union's biodiversity strategies or African Union initiatives on land and water management, complement global frameworks by tailoring them to specific ecological and socio-economic contexts. These agreements demonstrate how international policy frameworks can be adapted to regional realities while maintaining coherence with global goals.

Despite their importance, international frameworks face challenges in implementation and enforcement. Many commitments are voluntary or lack strong compliance mechanisms, leading to gaps between pledges and actual progress. Financial and technical capacity in many countries remains limited, creating disparities in how effectively natural capital is protected. Moreover, conflicting priorities—such as economic growth versus conservation—can undermine commitments. Ensuring coherence across different agreements also remains difficult, as biodiversity, climate, and trade policies are often negotiated separately despite their interconnectedness.

Nevertheless, international policy frameworks provide critical scaffolding for advancing natural capital globally. They establish shared norms, foster cooperation, and encourage integration of ecological considerations into economic and development planning. While implementation challenges persist, these frameworks remain essential for guiding national actions and mobilizing international support. As pressures on ecosystems intensify, their role in ensuring that natural capital is recognized and preserved at a global scale will only grow in importance.

National and Regional Policies

National and regional policies are essential for translating global frameworks on natural capital into concrete actions that reflect local ecological, economic, and cultural realities. While international agreements provide overarching goals and principles, it is at the national and regional levels where these ideas are operationalized through laws, regulations, strategies, and programs. Such policies not only determine how natural capital is valued and managed but also influence how benefits and responsibilities are distributed among different stakeholders. The diversity of approaches around the world illustrates both the opportunities and challenges of embedding natural capital into governance.

Many countries have developed national biodiversity strategies and action plans as part of their commitments under the Convention on Biological Diversity. These plans often include specific measures to conserve ecosystems, protect species, and integrate natural capital into development planning. For instance, governments may establish protected areas, promote sustainable land-use practices, or create incentives for ecosystem restoration. National strategies frequently emphasize mainstreaming biodiversity and natural capital across sectors such as agriculture, forestry, fisheries, and urban development, ensuring that ecological considerations are embedded in broader economic agendas.

Regional policies often complement and reinforce these national efforts. The European Union, for example, has developed an extensive suite of environmental policies that incorporate natural capital concepts. The EU Biodiversity Strategy, the Common Agricultural Policy, and the Water Framework Directive all aim to protect and enhance natural capital while promoting sustainable economic development. These policies require member states to monitor and report on ecosystem health, establish conservation areas, and ensure sustainable resource use. By creating legally binding obligations across multiple countries, the EU provides a model of regional integration that emphasizes accountability and cooperation.

In other regions, policies are shaped by specific ecological and socio-economic contexts. In Africa, initiatives under the African Union emphasize sustainable land and water management, recognizing the critical role of natural capital in supporting livelihoods, food security, and resilience to climate change. Programs such as the Great Green Wall initiative illustrate regional efforts to restore degraded lands while improving economic opportunities. In Asia, countries have adopted a range of policies to address rapid urbanization, deforestation, and marine resource depletion, with regional organizations promoting cooperation on shared resources like rivers and seas. Latin America has also pioneered innovative policies, particularly in relation to forests and indigenous rights, reflecting the region's rich biodiversity and cultural diversity.

National policies on natural capital often focus on integrating ecosystem values into economic planning and decision-making. Some governments have adopted natural capital accounting systems to measure the condition of ecosystems and their contributions to the economy. These accounts inform policy choices, such as balancing agricultural expansion with forest conservation or designing payment schemes for ecosystem services. Policy instruments also include subsidies for conservation practices, regulations limiting pollution, and tax incentives for sustainable resource use. By aligning economic incentives with ecological sustainability, these measures aim to ensure that natural capital is preserved while supporting development goals.

Decentralized governance structures further shape natural capital management. In many countries, local or regional governments play a significant role in implementing policies, especially where ecosystems cross administrative boundaries. For example, watershed management often requires coordination across municipalities or provinces to ensure sustainable water use. Regional authorities may also develop localized policies that reflect specific environmental challenges, such as coastal protection, desertification control, or urban greening. These localized approaches complement national strategies by addressing the unique dynamics of ecosystems at smaller scales.

Despite these advances, challenges remain. Policy implementation is often constrained by limited financial and technical capacity, particularly in developing countries. Conflicts between economic growth and environmental protection can undermine commitments, with short-term priorities outweighing long-term sustainability. Fragmentation across government agencies and sectors can also hinder coordination, leading to inconsistent or conflicting policies. Moreover, the integration of natural capital into economic planning often faces resistance from stakeholders who perceive conservation as a constraint on development. Addressing these barriers requires strong institutions, political will, and inclusive governance that engages diverse stakeholders.

National and regional policies are thus critical to advancing natural capital, translating international commitments into tangible outcomes. They reflect the diversity of ecological conditions and governance structures around the world, while also highlighting common challenges of implementation, coordination, and balance. By strengthening these policies and ensuring they are effectively enforced, countries and regions can safeguard their natural capital, securing the foundation for sustainable development and resilience in the face of global environmental change.

Institutional Roles and Responsibilities

The effective management of natural capital requires clearly defined institutional roles and responsibilities at multiple levels of governance. Institutions provide the frameworks within which natural assets are valued, conserved, and used, ensuring that policies and actions are coordinated and sustainable. These roles span international organizations, national governments, subnational authorities, private sector actors, and civil society, each contributing distinct capacities and perspectives. Understanding how responsibilities are allocated across institutions is central to creating coherent approaches to natural capital management.

At the international level, multilateral organizations set norms and standards that guide national and regional policies. The United Nations plays a leading role, particularly through agencies such as the United Nations Environment Programme, which supports countries in developing strategies for biodiversity conservation, ecosystem restoration, and environmental governance. Institutions like the World Bank and regional development banks promote the integration of natural capital into economic planning by providing technical assistance, capacity-building, and financing. Global conventions, including the Convention on Biological Diversity and the United Nations Framework Convention on Climate Change, assign responsibilities to signatory countries, creating obligations for monitoring, reporting, and action. These institutions provide the overarching architecture within which natural capital is recognized and prioritized.

National governments hold primary responsibility for translating international commitments into domestic policy and practice. They establish legislation, regulatory frameworks, and financial mechanisms to protect and manage ecosystems. Ministries of environment, forestry, agriculture, water, and energy are typically tasked with implementing policies that directly affect natural capital, while ministries of finance and planning play crucial roles in integrating ecological considerations into economic systems. Governments also oversee national accounting systems, including natural capital accounts that measure the status of resources and ecosystem services. Coordination across ministries is critical, as natural capital issues often cut across traditional administrative boundaries, requiring integrated approaches to land use, water management, and climate adaptation.

Subnational authorities and local governments also play key roles, particularly where natural capital management requires place-based approaches. Regional or municipal institutions are often responsible for land-use planning, water resource management, and urban development. Local governments may oversee protected areas, manage waste and pollution, and design green infrastructure projects that enhance urban natural capital. Their proximity to communities allows them to respond to local needs and priorities, while their ability to enforce regulations and implement projects ensures that broader national strategies are grounded in local realities. Decentralization can enhance accountability and responsiveness, though it also creates challenges of capacity and resource allocation.

The private sector is increasingly recognized as a critical actor in natural capital management. Corporations and investors both depend on and impact natural assets through their operations and supply chains. Institutions such as industry associations, financial regulators, and stock exchanges are beginning to require or encourage disclosure of natural capital risks and dependencies. Tools like the Natural Capital Protocol provide businesses with frameworks for assessing their impacts, while financial institutions develop instruments that align investments with ecological sustainability. By incorporating natural capital into corporate strategies and financial reporting, the private sector assumes responsibility not only for compliance but also for innovation in conservation and sustainable resource use.

Civil society, including non-governmental organizations, community groups, and indigenous institutions, provides advocacy, oversight, and direct management of natural capital. NGOs often act as watchdogs, holding governments and businesses accountable for environmental commitments. They also implement conservation projects, conduct research, and raise public awareness of natural capital issues. Indigenous peoples and local communities, whose livelihoods and cultural identities are often directly tied to natural systems, play a vital role in stewardship. Their traditional knowledge and practices contribute to the sustainable management of ecosystems, while their participation in governance enhances legitimacy and inclusivity. Strengthening the roles of these actors is essential for ensuring that natural capital policies respect diverse values and rights.

Effective governance of natural capital depends on coordination across these institutional levels and actors. Fragmentation of responsibilities can undermine progress, as conflicting mandates or lack of communication create inefficiencies and gaps. Strong institutions must therefore establish mechanisms for collaboration, data sharing, and conflict resolution. Clear allocation of roles—international bodies setting norms, national governments establishing frameworks, subnational authorities implementing place-based actions, private actors innovating and disclosing, and civil society advocating and managing—creates a balanced system of shared responsibility. Such arrangements ensure that natural capital is safeguarded and enhanced as a foundation for sustainable development.

Challenges in Implementation

Despite the growing recognition of natural capital as a framework for integrating ecological assets into economic and policy decisions, significant challenges arise in implementation. These challenges are technical, institutional, financial, and cultural in nature, often creating barriers that slow progress or limit effectiveness. Understanding these obstacles is crucial to improving strategies for safeguarding natural assets and ensuring that the benefits of natural capital approaches are realized.

One of the foremost challenges is the complexity of ecosystems and the difficulty of measurement. Natural systems are dynamic, interdependent, and influenced by numerous variables, making it difficult to capture their full value through accounting frameworks. While some ecosystem services, such as timber production or water supply, can be measured with relative ease, others, including cultural services or biodiversity's role in resilience, are harder to quantify. The reliance on incomplete or uncertain data can lead to undervaluation, misrepresentation, or misinformed decisions. This measurement gap is compounded by limited technical capacity in many countries, particularly those with high biodiversity but constrained resources for ecological monitoring.

Another challenge lies in institutional fragmentation. Natural capital management typically spans multiple sectors—forestry, water, agriculture, energy, finance—each governed by different agencies with their own mandates and priorities. Coordination between ministries or departments is often weak, resulting in overlapping policies, inconsistent goals, or even contradictory actions. For instance, one agency may promote agricultural expansion while another advocates forest conservation, creating conflicts that undermine natural capital objectives. Institutional silos can also lead to inefficient use of resources, as agencies duplicate efforts or fail to share information. Addressing these governance gaps requires stronger mechanisms for cross-sectoral integration and accountability.

Financial and economic barriers also complicate implementation. Although natural capital frameworks emphasize the long-term economic value of ecosystems, short-term economic incentives often drive decisions. Governments may prioritize immediate growth, infrastructure expansion, or extractive industries over conservation, particularly when fiscal pressures are high. Similarly, businesses may struggle to justify investments in natural capital if financial returns are uncertain or delayed. Limited funding for conservation, restoration, and natural capital accounting further constrains progress. While international funding mechanisms and market-based instruments are emerging, they remain unevenly distributed and insufficient relative to the scale of ecological challenges.

Cultural and ethical considerations present another layer of difficulty. Natural capital approaches often frame ecosystems in economic terms, emphasizing their contribution to human well-being and financial systems. This can clash with worldviews that see nature as possessing intrinsic value, beyond human use. Indigenous peoples and local communities, for example, may resist frameworks that commodify resources central to their cultural and spiritual identity. Failure to respect these perspectives risks marginalizing traditional knowledge, undermining local governance, and creating social tensions. Inclusive approaches that recognize both economic and non-economic values are necessary to ensure legitimacy and fairness.

Policy inertia and political constraints further limit implementation. Integrating natural capital into decision-making often requires significant reforms, from revising national accounts to restructuring subsidies and regulations. These reforms can face resistance from entrenched interests, particularly industries that benefit from resource-intensive models of growth. Political cycles also discourage long-term planning, as governments prioritize policies with immediate benefits over those addressing future risks. In some cases, weak enforcement of environmental laws allows natural capital degradation to continue despite formal commitments. Building political will and public support is therefore essential for overcoming these barriers.

Global inequalities complicate the picture. Many of the world's most critical ecosystems are located in developing countries, which often face limited capacity for monitoring, valuation, and governance of natural capital. At the same time, wealthier nations and global markets exert significant demand pressures on these ecosystems through trade and consumption. This imbalance creates a challenge of fairness: developing countries may bear the costs of conserving natural capital while others reap disproportionate benefits. Mechanisms for international cooperation, capacity-building, and equitable financing are crucial to addressing these disparities.

Chapter 4: Business and Finance Perspectives

Business and finance perspectives on natural capital highlight the growing recognition that ecosystems underpin corporate performance, market stability, and long-term economic resilience. Companies depend on natural assets for resources, supply chain continuity, and risk management, while financial markets are increasingly exposed to nature-related risks. By incorporating natural capital into corporate strategies, firms can identify dependencies, manage risks, and seize opportunities in emerging green markets. Likewise, investors and financial institutions are beginning to account for natural capital in disclosure frameworks, lending practices, and portfolio management. These perspectives demonstrate how aligning finance with ecological sustainability supports resilient growth.

Corporate Natural Capital Accounting

Corporate natural capital accounting is a framework through which businesses measure, assess, and disclose their dependencies on and impacts upon natural systems. Companies rely heavily on resources such as water, energy, raw materials, and ecosystem services, yet these dependencies are often invisible in conventional financial accounts. By incorporating natural capital into their reporting, businesses can better understand risks, identify opportunities, and align operations with sustainability goals. The practice bridges the gap between ecological realities and corporate decision-making, ensuring that long-term resilience and profitability are considered alongside short-term financial performance.

One of the main purposes of corporate natural capital accounting is to make the hidden value of ecosystems visible. Traditional financial accounts track produced and financial capital but rarely reflect the costs of environmental degradation or the benefits ecosystems provide. For example, a company that depends on clean water for production may not account for the ecosystem services of the watershed that supplies it. By creating accounts that track both stocks and flows of natural capital, businesses can recognize these contributions and incorporate them into operational and strategic planning. This enhances transparency and allows companies to communicate the full scope of their value creation to investors and stakeholders.

Different frameworks and tools have been developed to guide businesses in implementing natural capital accounting. The Natural Capital Protocol, created by the Natural Capital Coalition, provides a standardized process for companies to measure and value their impacts and dependencies. It encourages businesses to define scope, identify priority natural capital issues, measure changes in ecosystems, and value those changes in monetary or non-monetary terms. Other approaches include ecosystem service valuation models, environmental profit and loss accounts, and integrated reporting that links natural, social, and financial capital. These tools offer flexibility to companies across sectors, allowing them to tailor methods to their specific industries and contexts.

Corporate natural capital accounting supports risk management by helping firms identify vulnerabilities in supply chains and operations. For example, an agricultural company may discover that its reliance on pollination services creates exposure to declines in pollinator populations. A beverage company may find that water scarcity poses a risk to its production facilities. Recognizing these dependencies enables companies to anticipate disruptions, adapt strategies, and build resilience. At the same time, natural capital accounting can highlight opportunities, such as the financial benefits of investing in ecosystem restoration, improving resource efficiency, or developing sustainable products that appeal to environmentally conscious consumers.

Another dimension of corporate natural capital accounting is its role in investor relations and regulatory compliance. Investors are increasingly demanding information on environmental risks and sustainability performance, recognizing that natural capital issues can influence long-term returns. Disclosure frameworks, such as those promoted by the Task Force on Nature-related Financial Disclosures, are gaining traction, requiring businesses to provide systematic information on their environmental impacts and dependencies. By adopting natural capital accounting, companies can meet these expectations, improve credibility with stakeholders, and demonstrate leadership in sustainability. In some jurisdictions, regulations are beginning to require companies to disclose environmental information, further embedding natural capital into corporate governance.

Despite these benefits, challenges remain in the widespread adoption of corporate natural capital accounting. Measuring and valuing ecosystem services is complex, and many businesses lack the expertise or data to conduct comprehensive assessments. There is also the risk that companies may adopt superficial approaches, using natural capital accounting as a public relations exercise rather than a genuine tool for sustainability. Ensuring consistency and comparability across companies is another challenge, as different sectors and regions face unique ecological and economic contexts. Overcoming these obstacles requires collaboration across industry, government, and academia to develop robust methods, build capacity, and standardize reporting practices.

Corporate natural capital accounting is emerging as a powerful tool for embedding ecological considerations into business decision-making. By identifying dependencies, valuing ecosystem services, and disclosing risks and impacts, companies can align financial performance with environmental stewardship. As pressures on ecosystems intensify and stakeholder expectations grow, businesses that integrate natural capital into their operations and reporting are better positioned to ensure resilience, competitiveness, and legitimacy in a rapidly changing world.

Financial Instruments and Markets

Financial instruments and markets have become important mechanisms for channeling investment into the protection and enhancement of natural capital. By translating ecological value into financial products, these tools create pathways for aligning economic incentives with environmental sustainability. They enable investors, businesses, and governments to mobilize capital for conservation, restoration, and sustainable use of natural resources, while also managing risks associated with environmental degradation. The development of such instruments reflects a growing recognition that financial systems and ecological systems are deeply interconnected.

One major category of financial instruments linked to natural capital is green bonds. These are fixed-income securities issued to finance projects with environmental benefits, such as renewable energy, reforestation, or water management. Green bonds provide investors with stable returns while directing capital toward sustainability goals. Over the past decade, the market for green bonds has expanded significantly, supported by standards and taxonomies that ensure transparency and accountability. By earmarking funds for environmentally beneficial activities, green bonds connect investor demand for sustainable assets with the financing needs of natural capital projects.

Sustainability-linked bonds and loans represent another innovative class of instruments. Unlike green bonds, which are tied to specific projects, these instruments link the financial terms of lending to the sustainability performance of the issuer. For example, a company may receive favorable interest rates if it meets targets for reducing emissions, conserving water, or protecting ecosystems. This approach incentivizes firms to integrate natural capital considerations into core business operations, not just isolated projects. The flexibility of these instruments allows for broader engagement across industries, making them a powerful driver of change in corporate behavior.

Markets for ecosystem services have also gained traction as mechanisms for valuing and trading ecological benefits. Carbon markets are the most established example, enabling the trading of credits generated from activities such as afforestation, soil carbon sequestration, or wetland restoration. These markets create financial incentives for protecting ecosystems that act as carbon sinks. Similarly, water quality trading schemes allow entities to purchase credits generated by upstream conservation efforts that improve water quality downstream. Biodiversity offset markets are emerging in some regions, where developers compensate for habitat loss by financing restoration or conservation elsewhere. These markets integrate natural capital into economic systems by assigning tradable value to ecosystem services.

Insurance products are increasingly being designed to incorporate natural capital. Parametric insurance schemes, for instance, provide payouts when environmental thresholds are crossed, such as flood levels or storm intensity. By linking insurance products to ecosystem services, such as mangroves that reduce storm surges or reefs that protect coastlines, financial markets can incentivize ecosystem preservation. These approaches reduce disaster risk while recognizing the protective value of natural capital. In addition, environmental risk insurance products help businesses and governments manage liabilities related to ecological degradation, reinforcing the financial case for sustainable practices.

The role of financial markets extends beyond individual instruments to broader portfolio management and investment strategies. Asset managers are increasingly considering natural capital risks and opportunities in their decision-making, recognizing that environmental degradation poses systemic threats to long-term returns. ESG (environmental, social, and governance) frameworks have evolved to include natural capital considerations, encouraging investors to assess corporate dependencies on ecosystems and biodiversity. Stock exchanges and regulators are also playing a role by promoting disclosure standards and sustainability indices that highlight companies with strong natural capital performance.

Despite these advances, challenges remain in scaling up financial instruments and markets for natural capital. Valuation uncertainties, lack of standardized methodologies, and data gaps hinder the development of reliable metrics. Concerns about greenwashing— where financial products are marketed as sustainable without delivering meaningful impact—undermine investor confidence. Regulatory frameworks vary across jurisdictions, creating inconsistencies that limit market growth. Furthermore, many natural capital benefits are localized or non-substitutable, complicating efforts to create tradable markets that capture their full value. Overcoming these barriers requires continued innovation, robust governance, and collaboration among financial institutions, governments, and civil society.

Financial instruments and markets linked to natural capital represent an important frontier in aligning finance with sustainability. By creating mechanisms that value and reward ecological stewardship, they connect the priorities of investors with the imperatives of environmental protection. Their continued evolution will be critical in mobilizing the scale of capital required to maintain and restore the natural systems upon which economies and societies depend.

Integrating Natural Capital Into Investment Decisions

Integrating natural capital into investment decisions involves recognizing the value of ecosystems and biodiversity as critical factors influencing financial performance and long-term stability. Investors and financial institutions are increasingly aware that environmental degradation poses material risks to portfolios, while sustainable management of natural assets can create new opportunities. By embedding natural capital considerations into investment strategies, asset managers and businesses can better align financial goals with ecological resilience.

A key driver of integration is the growing recognition of nature-related risks. Environmental degradation can disrupt supply chains, reduce resource availability, and create liabilities for companies that rely heavily on ecosystems. For instance, industries such as agriculture, forestry, fisheries, and energy are directly dependent on water, soil fertility, and biodiversity. Depletion of these resources can reduce yields, increase costs, and undermine profitability. Even sectors less directly connected to natural resources face risks, as climate change, water scarcity, and biodiversity loss create systemic challenges that ripple through economies and markets. Investors who ignore these risks may underestimate the long-term vulnerability of their assets.

Integrating natural capital into investment decisions also provides opportunities for identifying growth sectors. Markets for renewable energy, sustainable agriculture, water efficiency technologies, and ecosystem restoration are expanding as demand for environmentally responsible solutions rises. By assessing natural capital, investors can identify companies and projects positioned to benefit from these trends. Investments that contribute to ecosystem preservation or restoration may yield both financial returns and reputational benefits, appealing to stakeholders who prioritize sustainability. This alignment of financial and ecological outcomes reflects a shift toward investments that generate multiple forms of value.

Practical integration requires tools and frameworks for measuring and valuing natural capital. ESG criteria have traditionally guided responsible investment, but there is growing recognition that ESG must evolve to explicitly address dependencies on ecosystems. New initiatives, such as the Task Force on Nature-related Financial Disclosures, provide guidelines for assessing and reporting on nature-related risks and opportunities. Natural capital accounting frameworks, scenario analysis, and ecosystem service valuation models are also being adopted to quantify impacts and dependencies. These tools enable investors to integrate ecological considerations into financial models, portfolio analysis, and risk assessments.

Portfolio diversification and resilience are enhanced when natural capital is considered in investment strategies. For example, investors may avoid overexposure to sectors vulnerable to water scarcity or resource depletion, while increasing exposure to companies developing sustainable alternatives. By integrating ecosystem risks into financial analysis, investors can reduce volatility and protect long-term returns. In addition, alignment with global sustainability goals, such as the Paris Agreement and the Sustainable Development

Goals, positions portfolios to benefit from regulatory shifts, market incentives, and consumer preferences favoring sustainability.

Engagement with companies is another pathway for integrating natural capital into investment decisions. Investors can encourage firms to assess their natural capital dependencies, disclose relevant information, and adopt sustainable practices. Shareholder activism, voting policies, and sustainability-linked financing all serve as mechanisms to influence corporate behavior. By pressing companies to account for their impacts and risks, investors not only protect their portfolios but also contribute to broader ecological resilience. This collaborative approach bridges the gap between finance and environmental stewardship.

Challenges remain in fully integrating natural capital into investment practices. Valuation of ecosystem services is complex, with uncertainties in data and methodologies. Not all benefits and risks can be easily monetized, raising the possibility of underestimating nature's role. Consistency and comparability across disclosures are also limited, making it difficult to assess performance across companies and sectors. Furthermore, short-term financial pressures often outweigh long-term sustainability considerations, creating tensions for investors seeking immediate returns. Addressing these challenges requires continued innovation in measurement, stronger regulatory frameworks, and greater collaboration among financial institutions, governments, and civil society.

Integrating natural capital into investment decisions is a dynamic and evolving process. It reflects a growing recognition that ecosystems are not external to economies but foundational to them. By aligning financial systems with ecological sustainability, investors can reduce risks, unlock opportunities, and contribute to the preservation of the natural assets that underpin long-term prosperity.

Risks and Opportunities for Businesses

The concept of natural capital presents both risks and opportunities for businesses across all sectors of the economy. Companies depend on natural systems for resources, services, and resilience, but they also contribute to their degradation through pollution, overextraction, and land-use change. As recognition of these dynamics grows, businesses face increasing pressure from regulators, investors, consumers, and communities to account for their impacts and dependencies on natural capital. How companies respond to these pressures can expose them to risks or position them to seize emerging opportunities.

A central risk for businesses is the degradation of ecosystems upon which they rely. Industries such as agriculture, forestry, fisheries, and mining are directly dependent on natural resources, while sectors such as manufacturing and energy rely heavily on water, soil fertility, and climate regulation. If these resources become scarce or degraded, businesses may experience higher costs, reduced productivity, and increased volatility. For example, water scarcity can disrupt production processes, while declining soil quality can undermine agricultural yields. Even industries less directly tied to natural systems, such as finance and insurance, face systemic risks as climate change, biodiversity loss, and resource depletion create economic instability.

Regulatory and compliance risks are also significant. Governments around the world are strengthening environmental regulations to protect natural capital, from stricter pollution controls and land-use restrictions to requirements for disclosure of environmental impacts. Businesses that fail to comply with these regulations face fines, legal liabilities, and reputational damage. Moreover, new policies such as carbon pricing or biodiversity offset requirements can increase operational costs, particularly for resource-intensive industries. Companies that anticipate and adapt to these regulatory shifts are better positioned to manage risks, while those that lag may find themselves at a competitive disadvantage.

Reputational risks are another critical concern. As consumers, investors, and civil society become more aware of environmental issues, companies are increasingly judged by their environmental performance. Negative publicity surrounding resource depletion, pollution, or ecosystem destruction can erode brand value and consumer trust. This is particularly acute in industries that market themselves on sustainability credentials, such as food, apparel, or tourism. Social media amplifies reputational risks, as campaigns can quickly mobilize public opinion against businesses seen as irresponsible. Companies that integrate natural capital into their strategies can instead build reputational strength by demonstrating environmental stewardship.

Financial risks related to natural capital are becoming more visible. Investors are beginning to recognize that ecological degradation poses material threats to long-term returns. Asset managers are incorporating natural capital into their risk assessments, and financial regulators are exploring disclosure requirements. Businesses that fail to disclose their dependencies and impacts may struggle to attract investment or face higher costs of capital. Insurance companies are also factoring natural capital into risk models, adjusting premiums to reflect exposure to environmental hazards. As financial systems integrate ecological considerations, businesses that ignore natural capital risk losing access to affordable financing and insurance.

Despite these risks, opportunities for businesses are also expanding as natural capital becomes a central focus of sustainability. One opportunity lies in efficiency improvements. By reducing resource use, minimizing waste, and adopting circular economy principles, companies can lower costs while reducing environmental impacts. Advances in water efficiency, renewable energy, and sustainable materials are already creating competitive advantages for firms that invest in them. These efficiencies not only protect natural capital but also enhance resilience in the face of resource scarcity.

Innovation is another major opportunity. Businesses that develop products and services supporting ecosystem restoration, sustainable agriculture, renewable energy, or green infrastructure are well positioned to capture growing demand for environmentally responsible solutions. Nature-based solutions, such as reforestation or wetland restoration, are gaining traction as cost-effective ways to address climate and biodiversity challenges. Companies that pioneer such solutions can diversify revenue streams while contributing to ecological sustainability.

Market opportunities also arise from shifting consumer preferences. Consumers are increasingly willing to pay for products and services that reflect sustainable practices and responsible sourcing. Certification schemes, eco-labels, and transparency initiatives help businesses differentiate themselves and build loyalty among environmentally conscious customers. This trend is evident across sectors, from sustainable food and fashion to eco-tourism and renewable energy. Companies that embrace natural capital in their value propositions can gain market share and strengthen customer relationships.

Finally, businesses can benefit from improved relationships with stakeholders by integrating natural capital into their strategies. Engaging with local communities, indigenous groups, and civil society organizations fosters trust and collaboration, reducing conflict over resource use. Partnerships with governments and NGOs can also create opportunities for co-investment in conservation and restoration projects. These collaborations enhance social license to operate and provide access to expertise, funding, and new markets.

The interplay of risks and opportunities highlights the strategic importance of natural capital for businesses. Companies that fail to address their dependencies and impacts face operational, financial, and reputational risks, while those that integrate natural capital into decision-making can unlock innovation, efficiency, and market growth. Recognizing and managing this balance is essential for long-term competitiveness in a world where ecological sustainability is increasingly inseparable from economic success.

Chapter 5: Terrestrial Ecosystems and Land Use

Terrestrial ecosystems and patterns of land use play a defining role in shaping the availability and quality of natural capital. Forests, grasslands, agricultural lands, and drylands not only provide food, fiber, and raw materials but also regulate climate, store carbon, filter water, and support biodiversity. How societies choose to manage and transform land has direct implications for ecological integrity, economic productivity, and human well-being.

This chapter explores the interplay between terrestrial ecosystems and land use, examining how competing demands for agriculture, forestry, conservation, and urban expansion influence natural capital. It highlights pathways for balancing development needs with ecological sustainability.

Forests as Natural Capital

Forests represent one of the most critical components of natural capital, providing a wide range of goods and services that sustain ecological balance, support economic development, and enhance human well-being. They cover approximately one-third of the Earth's land area and harbor more than half of all terrestrial species. Their contributions extend far beyond timber and non-timber products, encompassing climate regulation, water cycle maintenance, soil protection, and cultural and recreational values. Recognizing forests as natural capital underscores their role as both ecological assets and economic foundations that require careful stewardship.

One of the most visible functions of forests as natural capital is their role in provisioning goods. Timber, fuelwood, fruits, nuts, resins, and medicinal plants are among the many resources derived directly from forest ecosystems. These resources support local livelihoods, national economies, and global trade. For many rural communities, forests provide subsistence needs and act as safety nets during times of hardship. The economic value of forest products is significant, yet these benefits represent only a fraction of the total contributions forests make to society.

Forests play a central role in regulating ecological processes, making them invaluable natural capital assets. They act as major carbon sinks, absorbing vast amounts of carbon dioxide and mitigating the impacts of climate change. Their role in water regulation is equally important: forests influence rainfall patterns, recharge groundwater, and maintain the stability of river systems. They reduce the risks of floods and droughts by regulating runoff and improving water quality through natural filtration processes. Forests also stabilize soils, prevent erosion, and support nutrient cycling, ensuring long-term fertility for agriculture and other land uses.

Biodiversity is another key dimension of forest natural capital. Forests provide habitat for a wide array of plant and animal species, supporting intricate ecological interactions that maintain ecosystem health. Tropical rainforests, in particular, are hotspots of biodiversity, containing a vast share of global species richness. This diversity underpins ecosystem resilience, allowing forests to adapt to disturbances such as disease, pests, or climate variability. It also contributes to human well-being by supporting genetic resources that have applications in agriculture, medicine, and biotechnology.

Forests also generate significant cultural and social values. They hold spiritual significance for many indigenous peoples and local communities, forming the basis of cultural identity, traditions, and practices. Forest landscapes provide spaces for recreation, tourism, and aesthetic appreciation, contributing to physical and mental health. In many societies, forests are integral to narratives of heritage and identity, reinforcing their value beyond material goods. These cultural services highlight the multifaceted role of forests as natural capital that sustains both tangible and intangible aspects of human life.

Despite their immense contributions, forests as natural capital face severe pressures. Deforestation, driven by agricultural expansion, logging, mining, and infrastructure development, continues at alarming rates in many regions. Climate change adds further stress, increasing the frequency of forest fires, pest outbreaks, and droughts. Unsustainable exploitation of forest resources depletes natural stocks, undermining the flows of services they provide. These challenges not only diminish biodiversity but also erode the ability of forests to regulate climate, support water cycles, and sustain human livelihoods.

Efforts to safeguard forests as natural capital include conservation policies, sustainable forest management practices, and restoration initiatives. Protected areas help conserve biodiversity and ecosystem services, while certification schemes promote sustainable timber and non-timber production. Reforestation and afforestation projects aim to restore degraded landscapes and enhance carbon sequestration. Increasingly, mechanisms such as payments for ecosystem services and carbon markets provide financial incentives for maintaining forest natural capital. These measures recognize that preserving forests is both an ecological necessity and an economic opportunity.

Forests as natural capital embody the interconnectedness of ecological systems, economies, and societies. They supply goods, regulate critical processes, harbor biodiversity, and provide cultural meaning. Their degradation undermines not only environmental sustainability but also economic and social stability. Treating forests as assets to be managed, valued, and restored ensures that they continue to provide essential services for present and future generations.

Agricultural Landscapes

Agricultural landscapes are a vital component of natural capital, providing food, fiber, and raw materials that sustain human societies while shaping ecological systems and cultural identities. These landscapes encompass croplands, pastures, agroforestry systems, and mosaic environments where human activity and ecosystems interact. As both producers of essential goods and providers of ecological services, agricultural landscapes highlight the dual role of natural capital in supporting economic activity and maintaining environmental stability.

The most immediate contribution of agricultural landscapes lies in their provisioning services. Croplands produce cereals, fruits, vegetables, and oilseeds, while pastures and rangelands support livestock production. These outputs form the foundation of global food systems, feeding billions of people and sustaining livelihoods in rural communities. Beyond food, agricultural landscapes generate raw materials such as cotton, wool, and bioenergy crops, which contribute to industries ranging from textiles to renewable energy. The value of these goods is immense, yet agricultural landscapes provide far more than marketable products.

Agricultural systems also perform crucial regulating and supporting services that underpin ecological balance. Soil fertility, for example, is maintained through processes such as nutrient cycling, organic matter accumulation, and microbial activity. Pollination by bees, birds, and other species sustains crop yields, while natural pest control reduces reliance on chemical inputs. Agricultural landscapes help regulate water cycles, with practices like agroforestry and cover cropping enhancing infiltration, reducing runoff, and improving water quality. These functions demonstrate that well-managed agricultural systems are more than production sites; they are active participants in ecosystem processes that sustain productivity and resilience.

Biodiversity within agricultural landscapes adds another dimension to their role as natural capital. Traditional farming systems, such as mixed cropping or agroforestry, often support high levels of species richness compared to monocultures. Genetic diversity within crops and livestock breeds enhances resilience to pests, diseases, and climate variability. Landscapes that incorporate hedgerows, wetlands, and field margins provide habitats for pollinators, birds, and other wildlife, creating ecological corridors that connect larger

53

ecosystems. This integration of biodiversity contributes not only to ecological health but also to long-term agricultural sustainability.

Agricultural landscapes also hold deep cultural and social significance. Farming practices, crop varieties, and land management traditions are closely tied to cultural identities, rituals, and knowledge systems. Rural landscapes reflect historical interactions between people and nature, carrying heritage value for communities worldwide. They provide spaces for recreation, education, and aesthetic appreciation, enriching human well-being in ways that extend beyond material production. The cultural services of agricultural landscapes reinforce the idea that natural capital is multidimensional, blending ecological, economic, and social values.

Despite their importance, agricultural landscapes face significant pressures that threaten their sustainability. Intensive farming practices, characterized by heavy use of synthetic fertilizers, pesticides, and monocultures, often degrade soil health, reduce biodiversity, and pollute water systems. Expansion of agricultural land into forests, wetlands, and grasslands drives deforestation, habitat loss, and greenhouse gas emissions. Climate change exacerbates these challenges, increasing the frequency of droughts, floods, and temperature extremes that undermine productivity. These pressures not only reduce the ecological functions of agricultural landscapes but also jeopardize their ability to sustain human needs in the long term.

Strategies for sustaining agricultural landscapes as natural capital focus on practices that balance productivity with ecological stewardship. Sustainable agriculture approaches, such as conservation tillage, organic farming, and integrated pest management, aim to maintain soil health and reduce chemical inputs. Agroecology emphasizes the use of ecological principles to design resilient farming systems, while regenerative agriculture seeks to restore degraded lands through practices that build soil organic matter and enhance biodiversity. Policy instruments, including agri-environmental schemes and payments for ecosystem services, provide incentives for farmers to adopt practices that conserve natural capital. Emerging markets for sustainable food and fiber products further encourage shifts toward environmentally responsible production.

Agricultural landscapes represent one of the most prominent intersections of human activity and natural capital. They generate essential goods, sustain ecological functions, harbor biodiversity, and embody cultural values. Their degradation undermines both environmental and economic stability, while their sustainable management offers opportunities to align productivity with resilience. By recognizing agricultural landscapes as natural capital, societies can ensure that these working environments continue to support both human prosperity and ecological integrity.

Grasslands and Drylands

Grasslands and drylands are extensive ecosystems that form a crucial part of global natural capital. They cover vast areas across continents, ranging from the North American prairies and African savannas to the steppes of Eurasia and the arid deserts of Australia and the Middle East. These landscapes are often undervalued compared to forests or wetlands, yet they provide essential ecological functions, support diverse species, and sustain millions of people. Their role as natural capital extends across provisioning, regulating, supporting, and cultural services, making them indispensable to both ecological stability and human well-being.

Grasslands are characterized by open vegetation dominated by grasses and herbaceous plants, often interspersed with shrubs or scattered trees. They thrive in moderate climates with seasonal rainfall and are among the most productive terrestrial ecosystems. Drylands, on the other hand, encompass arid, semi-arid, and dry sub-humid zones where water availability is limited and drought is a recurring feature. Despite their low productivity compared to wetter ecosystems, drylands cover more than 40 percent of the Earth's land surface and support around two billion people. These landscapes illustrate the diversity of natural capital, with grasslands offering high productivity in favorable conditions and drylands demonstrating resilience in environments of scarcity.

Provisioning services from grasslands and drylands are vital for human societies. They serve as major grazing lands for livestock, supplying meat, milk, wool, and hides that sustain rural economies and global markets. Many staple foods and crops have origins in these regions, including wheat, barley, and millet. Drylands also provide raw materials such as fuelwood, medicinal plants, and fibers, which are critical for local communities with limited alternatives. In addition, they supply genetic resources that support crop and livestock breeding, helping improve resilience to pests, diseases, and climate variability. These provisioning roles illustrate how grasslands and drylands underpin food security and livelihoods.

The regulating and supporting services of these ecosystems are equally important. Grasslands act as significant carbon sinks, storing large amounts of organic carbon in their soils. This carbon storage helps mitigate climate change, especially when grasslands are well-managed and not degraded. Drylands contribute to climate regulation by maintaining albedo effects and influencing regional climate systems. Both ecosystems play essential roles in hydrological cycles, with vegetation helping to regulate water infiltration, reduce runoff, and minimize erosion. Soil fertility in these regions is maintained through nutrient cycling, while symbiotic relationships between plants and microbes sustain productivity under challenging conditions. By stabilizing soils and reducing desertification risks, these landscapes safeguard ecological integrity in regions prone to degradation.

Biodiversity is another dimension of natural capital in grasslands and drylands. Grasslands host migratory species such as bison, antelope, and wildebeest, alongside diverse bird populations. Drylands support unique flora and fauna adapted to arid conditions, including succulents, desert-adapted mammals, and reptiles. These species contribute to ecosystem resilience and provide ecological services such as pollination and pest control. Biodiversity within these ecosystems also holds cultural, scientific, and economic value, with genetic resources offering potential for medicine, agriculture, and biotechnology. Protecting biodiversity is critical for maintaining the long-term functionality of grasslands and drylands.

Cultural services from grasslands and drylands enrich human societies. They are central to the identities and traditions of many pastoralist and indigenous communities, whose livelihoods and cultural practices revolve around herding, grazing, and sustainable resource use. These landscapes inspire art, literature, and spiritual traditions, while also providing spaces for recreation and tourism. National parks, game reserves, and heritage sites in savannas, prairies, and deserts attract millions of visitors each year, generating income and strengthening connections between people and nature. The cultural values of grasslands and drylands highlight their significance beyond material benefits.

Despite their value, grasslands and drylands face severe threats. Overgrazing, unsustainable agricultural expansion, and deforestation have degraded vast areas, reducing productivity and increasing vulnerability to desertification. Climate change exacerbates these pressures by intensifying droughts, altering rainfall patterns, and driving temperature extremes. Soil erosion, loss of biodiversity, and declining water availability further undermine the capacity of these ecosystems to provide essential services. Many grasslands have been converted to croplands, while drylands are experiencing growing pressures from population growth and resource demands. The degradation of these ecosystems diminishes their role as natural capital, with consequences for both local communities and global sustainability.

Efforts to conserve and restore grasslands and drylands focus on sustainable land management and community-based approaches. Practices such as rotational grazing, agro-pastoral systems, reforestation, and water harvesting can help maintain productivity while reducing degradation. Policy frameworks, including the United Nations Convention to Combat Desertification, provide guidance for global cooperation in addressing challenges specific to drylands. Payment schemes for ecosystem services and ecotourism initiatives can create financial incentives for conservation, while research and monitoring improve understanding of these ecosystems' dynamics. By integrating ecological stewardship with economic and social priorities, strategies for grasslands and drylands can enhance their resilience and sustain their contributions to natural capital.

Grasslands and drylands demonstrate the diversity and adaptability of natural capital across ecological contexts. They sustain food systems, regulate climate, support biodiversity, and enrich cultural heritage. Their vulnerabilities highlight the need for careful management and restoration, ensuring that their services are not irreversibly diminished. Recognizing their importance as natural capital provides a framework for balancing resource use with conservation, supporting both human prosperity and ecological resilience in some of the planet's most expansive and challenging environments.

Soil Systems and Nutrient Cycles

Soil systems are a fundamental component of natural capital, underpinning terrestrial ecosystems and agricultural productivity through their role in nutrient cycling, water regulation, and carbon storage. Soils are dynamic, living systems composed of minerals, organic matter, water, air, and countless microorganisms. These elements interact to create an environment that supports plant growth, decomposes organic material, filters pollutants, and stores essential nutrients. By maintaining the integrity of soil systems and their nutrient cycles, societies sustain the productivity of landscapes and ensure ecological stability.

Nutrient cycling is one of the most critical services provided by soil systems. It refers to the continuous movement and transformation of nutrients such as nitrogen, phosphorus, potassium, and carbon within ecosystems. Microorganisms, fungi, and soil fauna break down organic matter into simpler compounds that plants can absorb. These nutrients are then incorporated into plant tissues, consumed by herbivores, transferred through food webs, and eventually returned to the soil through waste and decomposition. This cyclical process ensures that nutrients are recycled rather than lost, maintaining soil fertility and supporting long-term ecosystem productivity.

Soil systems also play a pivotal role in carbon cycling. Organic matter in soils stores vast amounts of carbon, making soils one of the largest carbon reservoirs on Earth. Carbon enters soil through plant roots, litter, and microbial activity, and it is stored as organic compounds that can remain for decades or even centuries. This carbon storage helps regulate the global climate by reducing the concentration of carbon dioxide in the atmosphere. However, unsustainable practices such as deforestation, overgrazing, and intensive agriculture can release stored carbon, contributing to greenhouse gas emissions and climate change. Protecting soil carbon stocks is therefore critical for both food security and climate mitigation.

Water regulation is another essential function of soil systems. Soils act as sponges, absorbing rainfall, filtering it, and slowly releasing it into groundwater and rivers. This process reduces flood risk, maintains water quality, and provides steady supplies for agriculture and human consumption. Nutrient cycles are tightly linked to these hydrological processes, as water transports dissolved nutrients through soils and into plant roots. Excessive nutrient leaching, however, can degrade water quality, causing problems such as eutrophication in lakes and rivers. Effective soil management helps balance nutrient retention with water flow, ensuring that ecosystems and human communities benefit from clean and reliable water supplies.

Biodiversity within soils plays a central role in nutrient cycling. Bacteria, fungi, earthworms, insects, and other organisms form complex food webs that drive decomposition, mineralization, and nutrient exchange. For example, mycorrhizal fungi form symbiotic relationships with plant roots, enhancing the uptake of phosphorus and other nutrients. Nitrogen-fixing bacteria convert atmospheric nitrogen into forms usable by plants, sustaining fertility in many ecosystems. This hidden biodiversity illustrates the interconnectedness of soil systems and highlights the importance of maintaining soil health to preserve nutrient cycles.

Despite their importance, soil systems and nutrient cycles are under threat. Intensive agricultural practices, including monocultures, excessive fertilizer use, and heavy tillage, disrupt soil structure, deplete organic matter, and diminish microbial diversity. Over time, these practices lead to nutrient imbalances, reduced fertility, and increased reliance on synthetic inputs. Soil erosion, driven by deforestation, overgrazing, and poor land management, strips away nutrient-rich topsoil, further undermining ecosystem productivity. Climate change intensifies these pressures, altering precipitation patterns and increasing the frequency of droughts and floods that affect nutrient availability and soil stability.

Sustainable management of soil systems is essential to safeguard their role as natural capital. Practices such as conservation tillage, crop rotation, cover cropping, and agroforestry help maintain soil structure, enhance organic matter, and support nutrient cycling. The use of organic fertilizers and compost reduces dependence on synthetic inputs while enriching soil biodiversity. Integrated nutrient management approaches combine traditional knowledge with modern science to balance nutrient supply, reduce losses, and enhance efficiency. Policy frameworks and incentive programs, including payments for ecosystem services, can further encourage farmers and land managers to adopt practices that protect soils.

Soil systems and nutrient cycles are the foundation of terrestrial productivity, ecological balance, and climate regulation. By maintaining their health and resilience, societies ensure that natural capital continues to generate the food, water, and environmental stability needed for human and ecological well-being.

Chapter 6: Water and Marine Systems

Water and marine systems represent some of the most critical components of natural capital, sustaining life on Earth while regulating ecological and climatic processes. Freshwater ecosystems such as rivers, lakes, and wetlands provide drinking water, irrigation, sanitation, and hydropower, while coastal and marine environments support fisheries, biodiversity, and carbon storage. Together, these systems deliver essential services that underpin human health, food security, and economic prosperity.

This chapter examines the interconnections between freshwater and marine ecosystems, emphasizing their ecological functions, economic importance, and vulnerabilities to human pressures and climate change. It highlights the need for sustainable management that ensures resilience and long-term productivity.

Freshwater Ecosystems

Freshwater ecosystems are essential components of natural capital, encompassing rivers, lakes, streams, groundwater, and wetlands that provide life-sustaining resources and ecological services. Although they represent only a small fraction of Earth's water, these ecosystems are disproportionately important for biodiversity, climate regulation, and human well-being. They serve as habitats for countless species, supply water for agriculture and industry, and regulate ecological processes critical to the stability of landscapes and societies.

A primary contribution of freshwater ecosystems is their role in provisioning services. They provide drinking water, irrigation for crops, and water for industrial processes, supporting the foundations of human life and economic activity. Freshwater systems also sustain fisheries that supply protein to millions of people, particularly in developing countries. Beyond food and water, wetlands and rivers provide raw materials such as reeds, medicinal plants, and peat. These resources are vital for local livelihoods and global trade, making freshwater ecosystems integral to both subsistence and commercial economies.

Equally important are the regulating functions performed by freshwater ecosystems. Wetlands absorb and store floodwaters, reducing the severity of floods and protecting downstream communities. Rivers and lakes regulate hydrological flows, maintaining water availability during dry periods. Groundwater recharge areas replenish aquifers that provide long-term water security. Freshwater ecosystems also purify water by filtering pollutants, sediments, and excess nutrients, reducing the need for costly water treatment infrastructure. These regulating services highlight the economic and ecological value of intact freshwater systems.

Freshwater ecosystems are also crucial for biodiversity. They provide habitats for fish, amphibians, aquatic plants, invertebrates, and countless microorganisms. Many migratory species, such as salmon, storks, and waterfowl, depend on freshwater habitats during key stages of their life cycles. Wetlands and floodplains act as nurseries for fish and breeding grounds for birds. The diversity of life in freshwater ecosystems contributes to ecological resilience, ensuring that systems can adapt to disturbances such as climate change or pollution. Protecting biodiversity within these ecosystems safeguards the genetic resources that support agriculture, medicine, and biotechnology.

Cultural and social values add another dimension to the significance of freshwater ecosystems. Rivers, lakes, and wetlands are central to many spiritual traditions, cultural practices, and historical identities. They provide spaces for recreation, tourism, and aesthetic appreciation, contributing to mental and physical well-being. Popular activities such as boating, fishing, and swimming demonstrate the cultural services freshwater ecosystems offer. For many communities, these waterscapes are integral to cultural identity and heritage, reinforcing their value beyond material benefits.

Despite their importance, freshwater ecosystems face acute pressures. Pollution from agriculture, industry, and urban development degrades water quality, leading to eutrophication, habitat loss, and declining biodiversity. Overextraction of water for irrigation, hydropower, and industry disrupts ecological flows, drying out rivers and wetlands. Dams and infrastructure fragment habitats, altering sediment transport and blocking species migrations. Climate change compounds these stresses, with altered rainfall patterns, rising temperatures, and extreme weather events destabilizing freshwater systems. These pressures threaten not only ecological integrity but also the services upon which human societies depend.

Efforts to protect and restore freshwater ecosystems are expanding at global, national, and local levels. Integrated water resource management promotes the sustainable allocation of water across sectors while maintaining ecological flows. River restoration projects aim to reconnect floodplains, remove obsolete dams, and reestablish natural hydrological processes. Wetland conservation initiatives seek to preserve critical habitats and their biodiversity. Policies and international agreements, such as the Ramsar Convention on Wetlands, provide frameworks for coordinated action. Emerging financial instruments, including payments for ecosystem services and green infrastructure investments, support conservation while providing economic incentives for sustainable practices.

Freshwater ecosystems illustrate the interconnectedness of ecological health, human well-being, and economic stability. They provide vital resources, regulate critical processes, support rich biodiversity, and enrich cultural life. Their degradation undermines resilience and sustainability, while their restoration offers pathways to secure natural capital for future generations. Recognizing their value is essential for shaping policies and practices that balance human needs with ecological integrity.

Wetlands and Coastal Systems

Wetlands and coastal systems are vital elements of natural capital, providing ecological functions, economic value, and cultural significance. Wetlands include marshes, swamps, bogs, and peatlands, while coastal systems encompass estuaries, mangroves, salt marshes, coral reefs, and seagrass beds. These ecosystems act as transitional zones between land and water, supporting immense biodiversity and performing critical services that sustain both human societies and natural processes.

One of the defining features of wetlands and coastal systems is their role in regulating water flows. Wetlands act as natural sponges, absorbing excess rainfall and releasing it slowly, thereby reducing the severity of floods. They also recharge aquifers by allowing water to percolate into underground reserves. Coastal systems, particularly mangroves and salt marshes, buffer shorelines from storm surges, waves, and erosion, protecting human settlements and infrastructure. These functions demonstrate the regulating services of wetlands and coasts as natural barriers against increasingly severe climate-related hazards.

Water purification is another critical service. Wetlands filter pollutants, sediments, and nutrients from surface water, improving water quality for downstream users. Their vegetation and soils trap heavy metals, excess nitrogen, and phosphates, reducing risks of eutrophication in rivers and lakes. Coastal ecosystems provide similar benefits, with mangroves and seagrasses stabilizing sediments and reducing turbidity. These filtration services reduce the need for costly engineered water treatment systems, highlighting the economic efficiency of preserving wetlands and coastal natural capital.

Provisioning services add further value to these ecosystems. Wetlands support fisheries, providing breeding and nursery grounds for freshwater and marine species. They yield resources such as reeds, timber, peat, and medicinal plants, which are critical for local livelihoods. Coastal ecosystems sustain some of the world's most productive fisheries, including shrimp, crabs, and finfish. Coral reefs and seagrass beds support food security and tourism industries, generating employment and income. These provisioning roles illustrate how wetlands and coastal systems link ecological health with human prosperity.

Biodiversity within wetlands and coastal systems is remarkable. Wetlands host migratory birds, amphibians, and unique plants adapted to waterlogged conditions. Coastal ecosystems harbor species-rich environments, from mangrove forests teeming with invertebrates to coral reefs supporting thousands of fish species. These ecosystems act as genetic reservoirs, safeguarding resources that may have future applications in agriculture, medicine, and biotechnology. Their biodiversity enhances ecosystem resilience, ensuring continued provision of services under changing environmental conditions.

Cultural services also play an important role. Wetlands and coasts hold spiritual and cultural significance for many communities, often forming the basis of traditions, rituals, and identities. They provide recreational spaces for tourism, birdwatching, fishing, and water sports, contributing to mental and physical well-being. Coastal landscapes, in particular, are major attractions, with tourism centered on beaches, coral reefs, and estuaries contributing billions of dollars to global economies. These cultural dimensions highlight the multifaceted contributions of wetlands and coastal natural capital.

Despite their importance, wetlands and coastal systems are among the most threatened ecosystems on Earth. Draining wetlands for agriculture, urban expansion, and infrastructure development has led to significant losses worldwide. Pollution from agriculture, industry, and untreated sewage degrades water quality, reducing biodiversity and ecosystem functions. Overfishing and destructive practices such as trawling and mangrove clearing further stress coastal ecosystems. Climate change amplifies these threats, with sea level rise, ocean acidification, and intensified storms eroding coasts and altering wetland dynamics.

Conservation and restoration efforts aim to reverse these trends. International agreements, such as the Ramsar Convention on Wetlands, promote the protection of critical sites. Coastal management strategies integrate natural infrastructure, restoring mangroves and dunes to enhance resilience. Wetland restoration projects reestablish hydrological flows and biodiversity, improving ecological functions. Innovative financial instruments, such as payments for ecosystem services and blue carbon credits, incentivize the protection of wetlands and coastal systems. These approaches recognize the ecological, economic, and cultural value of these ecosystems as natural capital.

Wetlands and coastal systems are indispensable assets, sustaining water regulation, biodiversity, food production, and cultural values. Their degradation undermines ecological stability and human security, while their conservation offers cost-effective solutions for climate adaptation, food security, and sustainable development. Recognizing and protecting them as natural capital is central to ensuring that their benefits endure for future generations.

Oceans and Marine Resources

Oceans and marine resources are central to natural capital, providing vast ecological, economic, and cultural benefits that sustain life on Earth. Covering over 70 percent of the planet's surface, oceans regulate global climate, host extraordinary biodiversity, and supply resources essential for food security, trade, and human well-being. As natural capital, marine systems embody both tangible goods, such as fisheries and minerals, and intangible services, including carbon storage, nutrient cycling, and cultural values. Their scale and complexity make them among the most critical yet most threatened forms of natural capital.

One of the most important contributions of oceans is their role in regulating Earth's climate. Oceans act as massive carbon sinks, absorbing a significant proportion of atmospheric carbon dioxide and mitigating the pace of climate change. They also regulate temperature by storing and distributing heat through currents, which influence weather patterns and climate systems worldwide. Marine ecosystems such as mangroves, seagrasses, and salt marshes provide "blue carbon" storage, capturing carbon at rates much higher than terrestrial forests. These regulatory services highlight the indispensable role of oceans in maintaining planetary stability.

Provisioning services derived from marine resources are extensive. Fisheries provide protein for billions of people, particularly in coastal and island communities where alternatives may be limited. Oceans also supply raw materials such as salt, sand, oil, and gas, as well as emerging resources like deep-sea minerals critical for renewable energy technologies. Marine organisms contribute to pharmaceuticals, biotechnology, and cosmetics, demonstrating the economic importance of biodiversity within oceans. Tourism and recreation linked to marine environments, from coral reefs to coastal resorts, generate additional income and employment worldwide. These provisioning benefits make oceans central to both local livelihoods and global markets.

Biodiversity within marine ecosystems is unparalleled, with coral reefs, deep-sea vents, and open waters supporting diverse life forms adapted to a range of conditions. Marine biodiversity underpins ecological resilience, ensuring that ecosystems can adapt to changes such as climate variability or pollution. Species interactions contribute to nutrient cycling, food web stability, and habitat creation, such as reef-building corals or kelp forests. Genetic diversity within marine organisms offers opportunities for innovation in medicine, agriculture, and industry. The conservation of marine biodiversity is therefore integral to sustaining oceans as natural capital.

Cultural and social services provided by oceans and marine resources are equally significant. Oceans are central to cultural identities, spiritual practices, and traditional livelihoods of coastal and island communities. They inspire art, literature, and heritage, reinforcing their value beyond material benefits. Recreational and aesthetic enjoyment from marine environments contributes to physical and mental well-being, while marine tourism supports national economies. These cultural services highlight the multidimensional role of oceans in human societies.

Despite their immense value, oceans and marine resources face growing pressures. Overfishing threatens the sustainability of fish stocks and disrupts food webs. Destructive practices such as bottom trawling damage seabeds, while illegal and unregulated fishing undermines conservation efforts. Pollution from plastics, chemicals, and agricultural runoff degrades marine habitats, causing dead zones and harming wildlife. Climate change adds further stress, with warming waters, ocean acidification, and rising sea levels altering marine ecosystems and reducing resilience. These threats jeopardize not only biodiversity but also the ecosystem services upon which billions of people depend.

Efforts to protect oceans and marine resources include international agreements, national policies, and community-based initiatives. The United Nations Convention on the Law of the Sea provides a framework for managing marine resources and resolving disputes. Marine protected areas conserve biodiversity and sustain fisheries, while initiatives such as sustainable seafood certification promote responsible consumption. Innovations in marine governance, such as blue economy strategies, aim to align economic development with ecological sustainability. Emerging financial tools, including blue bonds and payments for ecosystem services, create incentives for protecting marine natural capital.

Oceans and marine resources illustrate the scale, richness, and fragility of natural capital. They regulate climate, sustain biodiversity, provide food and materials, and enrich human culture. Their degradation threatens ecological balance and human security, while their sustainable management offers opportunities to align environmental stewardship with economic prosperity. Recognizing oceans as natural capital underscores the need for global cooperation, sustainable practices, and long-term strategies that secure their benefits for future generations.

Fisheries and Aquatic Food Systems

Fisheries and aquatic food systems form a vital part of natural capital, linking ecological processes with food security, livelihoods, and cultural identity. These systems encompass marine and freshwater fisheries, aquaculture, and the broader supply chains that connect aquatic resources to global markets. They contribute not only to the provision of protein and essential nutrients but also to economic development, employment, and cultural heritage. As populations grow and demand for protein increases, the sustainable management of fisheries and aquatic food systems has become a pressing global priority.

Provisioning services are at the core of fisheries and aquatic food systems. Fish and other aquatic organisms provide one of the most important sources of animal protein worldwide, particularly in developing countries where alternatives may be scarce or expensive. In addition to protein, aquatic foods are rich in micronutrients such as omega-3 fatty acids, iron, and zinc, making them critical for nutritional security. Beyond fish, aquatic systems yield shellfish, crustaceans, seaweeds, and algae that contribute to diets and industries ranging from pharmaceuticals to cosmetics. Aquaculture, one of the fastest-growing food sectors, supplements wild fisheries by producing fish and other aquatic products in controlled environments. Together, these provisioning services demonstrate the central role of fisheries and aquatic food systems in sustaining human populations.

The economic importance of fisheries and aquaculture is substantial. Millions of people, particularly in coastal and riparian communities, depend on them for employment and income. Small-scale fisheries provide livelihoods for local communities, often employing more people than industrial fisheries. In many regions, they serve as social safety nets, offering income during times of economic or agricultural hardship. Global trade in fish and seafood contributes billions of dollars to national economies, with both developed and developing countries benefiting from exports. The financial value of these systems underscores their significance as natural capital that directly supports human prosperity.

Fisheries and aquatic food systems also deliver key regulating and supporting services. Healthy aquatic ecosystems regulate nutrient cycles, support carbon sequestration, and maintain hydrological balance. Mangroves, estuaries, and seagrass beds serve as nurseries for juvenile fish, sustaining population replenishment. Predatory species help regulate prey populations, maintaining ecosystem stability. These ecological functions highlight the interdependence of fisheries and the ecosystems that sustain them. When ecosystems are degraded, the productivity and resilience of fisheries decline, threatening food supplies and economic security.

Biodiversity is integral to the functioning of aquatic food systems. Genetic diversity within fish populations ensures resilience to diseases and environmental changes, while species diversity supports ecological balance. Coral reefs, wetlands, and rivers harbor diverse communities that underpin fisheries productivity. The loss of biodiversity, whether from overfishing, pollution, or habitat destruction, reduces the capacity of aquatic ecosystems to sustain food production. Conserving biodiversity within fisheries and aquatic food systems is therefore essential for maintaining their role as natural capital.

Cultural values add another layer of significance. Fisheries and aquatic resources are central to the traditions, identities, and practices of many communities. Fishing practices often carry historical and spiritual meanings, shaping local cultures and social structures. Aquatic foods are central to cuisines worldwide, representing cultural heritage and national identity. Recreational fishing and seafood-based tourism also contribute to cultural and economic life. These cultural services highlight the intangible value of fisheries and aquatic systems as part of natural capital.

Despite their importance, fisheries and aquatic food systems face significant pressures. Overfishing has depleted many fish stocks, while illegal, unreported, and unregulated fishing undermines sustainable management. Habitat destruction, pollution, and climate change compound these pressures, reducing the resilience of ecosystems and the productivity of fisheries. Aquaculture, while expanding food production, can contribute to environmental degradation if poorly managed, through nutrient pollution, disease spread, and habitat loss. These challenges jeopardize the sustainability of fisheries and their ability to continue providing essential services.

Efforts to ensure sustainability include international agreements, national regulations, and community-based management practices. Tools such as quotas, marine protected areas, and ecosystem-based management aim to balance exploitation with conservation. Certification schemes and traceability programs encourage sustainable consumption and trade. In aquaculture, innovations in feed, disease management, and ecological design reduce environmental impacts and enhance sustainability. Collaborative governance involving governments, businesses, and local communities is key to aligning ecological protection with food security and economic development.

Fisheries and aquatic food systems exemplify the integration of ecological processes, human nutrition, and economic activity. They provide food, employment, and cultural value while relying on the health and resilience of aquatic ecosystems. Ensuring their sustainability requires balancing current demands with the preservation of natural capital for future generations, recognizing that aquatic resources are both finite and indispensable.

Chapter 7: Natural Capital in Urban Environments

Urban environments present both challenges and opportunities for natural capital. As cities expand, ecosystems are often fragmented or replaced by built infrastructure, reducing the capacity of natural systems to provide essential services. Yet, urban areas also offer spaces where natural capital can be actively integrated into planning, design, and governance to enhance resilience, livability, and sustainability. Green infrastructure, biodiversity corridors, and ecosystem services in cities contribute to cleaner air and water, climate regulation, and public health benefits. This chapter explores the dynamics of natural capital in urban contexts, emphasizing its role in shaping sustainable and resilient cities.

Green Infrastructure and Ecosystem Services

Green infrastructure refers to strategically planned networks of natural and semi-natural areas designed to deliver a wide range of ecosystem services. Unlike traditional gray infrastructure, which relies on engineered solutions, green infrastructure uses natural processes and systems to provide services such as water regulation, climate mitigation, biodiversity conservation, and cultural enrichment. It encompasses features like parks, wetlands, urban forests, green roofs, and riparian corridors that enhance resilience while promoting sustainable development.

A central contribution of green infrastructure lies in regulating ecosystem services. Vegetation and soil systems within green spaces regulate water flows by absorbing rainfall, reducing runoff, and filtering pollutants. This decreases the risk of flooding, improves water quality, and reduces the need for costly stormwater infrastructure. Urban forests and green roofs also help regulate local climates by reducing the urban heat island effect, sequestering carbon, and improving air quality. These regulating services make green infrastructure an essential tool for adapting to climate change and enhancing urban resilience.

Green infrastructure provides vital provisioning services by supporting ecosystems that generate food, raw materials, and other resources. Community gardens, urban farms, and agroforestry systems produce fruits, vegetables, and medicinal plants. Wetlands and restored river corridors enhance fisheries and freshwater supplies. Although these contributions are often smaller in scale compared to industrial production, they add diversity, resilience, and accessibility to local food systems. In this way, green infrastructure connects ecological health with human well-being and livelihoods.

Supporting services are also integral to the role of green infrastructure. By maintaining soil fertility, promoting pollination, and sustaining habitat networks, green spaces enable ecosystems to function effectively and regenerate over time. Habitat corridors, for example, link fragmented ecosystems, allowing species to migrate, adapt, and maintain genetic diversity. This supports overall ecological resilience, ensuring that ecosystems continue to provide the services upon which human societies depend.

Cultural services add another dimension to the value of green infrastructure. Parks, urban forests, and waterfronts provide spaces for recreation, education, and aesthetic enjoyment. Access to green spaces is linked to improved physical and mental health, offering opportunities for exercise, relaxation, and social interaction. Green landscapes also carry cultural and heritage value, reflecting community identities and traditions. These cultural benefits highlight the multifaceted contributions of green infrastructure to human well-being.

The integration of green infrastructure into urban and regional planning is gaining momentum worldwide. Cities are increasingly recognizing the cost-effectiveness of nature-based solutions compared to conventional gray infrastructure. For example, green roofs and permeable pavements reduce stormwater runoff while enhancing urban biodiversity. Restored wetlands provide flood protection while serving as recreational and educational sites. Strategic investment in green infrastructure aligns economic, social, and environmental goals, creating co-benefits that extend across sectors.

Despite its benefits, implementing green infrastructure faces challenges. Limited funding, competing land uses, and lack of institutional coordination often hinder projects. Valuing ecosystem services in monetary terms remains complex, making it difficult to integrate green infrastructure into cost-benefit analyses. Social equity is another concern, as access to green spaces is often unevenly distributed across communities. Addressing these barriers requires supportive policies, cross-sector collaboration, and public engagement to ensure that green infrastructure benefits are shared equitably.

Green infrastructure demonstrates the potential of aligning human development with ecological processes. By providing ecosystem services ranging from flood control and carbon storage to recreation and cultural identity, it serves as a cornerstone of sustainable planning. Recognizing and investing in these systems as natural capital ensures that societies can meet current needs while safeguarding ecological resilience for the future.

Urban Biodiversity and Habitats

Urban biodiversity and habitats are increasingly recognized as crucial components of natural capital, even within landscapes dominated by human development. Cities are expanding rapidly, and with more than half of the world's population now living in urban areas, the ecological value of these spaces is gaining new significance. Urban biodiversity encompasses the variety of species, ecosystems, and ecological processes present in cities, while urban habitats include green spaces, rivers, wetlands, street trees, gardens, and even building surfaces. Together, they provide essential ecosystem services that enhance urban resilience, sustainability, and quality of life.

A key contribution of urban biodiversity lies in regulating ecosystem services. Vegetation in cities improves air quality by filtering pollutants and capturing particulates, while also sequestering carbon and mitigating the impacts of climate change. Urban habitats reduce the urban heat island effect, cooling local climates and lowering energy demand. Wetlands and riparian corridors manage stormwater by absorbing and filtering runoff, reducing flood risks. Pollinators thriving in urban gardens and parks support local food production, linking urban biodiversity directly to human health and food security. These regulating services highlight the importance of conserving and enhancing biodiversity even in densely built environments.

Urban biodiversity also contributes to provisioning services, albeit on a smaller scale compared to rural ecosystems. Community gardens, allotments, and rooftop farms provide fruits, vegetables, and medicinal plants, supporting local food systems and reducing dependence on imported produce. Trees and green spaces can yield timber, fiber, and other raw materials, although their role in provisioning is generally supplementary. The presence of diverse species within cities provides opportunities for education, research, and innovation in fields such as medicine, biotechnology, and sustainable design, further underscoring their value as natural capital.

Supporting services are equally vital in urban contexts. Biodiverse habitats maintain soil fertility, enable nutrient cycling, and support pollination and seed dispersal. Urban ecosystems also provide habitats for species that contribute to pest regulation, reducing the need for chemical control methods. Biodiversity within cities creates ecological networks that connect urban, peri-urban, and rural areas, allowing species to move, adapt, and sustain genetic diversity. These supporting services enhance ecological resilience, ensuring that urban environments remain functional and adaptable in the face of environmental change.

Cultural services provided by urban biodiversity and habitats are highly significant. Green spaces and urban wildlife enrich the quality of life by offering spaces for recreation, relaxation, and aesthetic enjoyment. Access to nature in cities is linked to improved physical and mental health, reducing stress and promoting social cohesion. Urban biodiversity also holds cultural and spiritual significance, with parks, rivers, and natural landmarks often serving as symbols of community identity and heritage. Educational opportunities abound in urban habitats, fostering environmental awareness and stewardship among residents. These cultural contributions emphasize that biodiversity in cities is not merely ornamental but integral to human well-being.

Despite these benefits, urban biodiversity faces considerable challenges. Habitat loss and fragmentation due to urban expansion are major threats, reducing the availability of green spaces and isolating species populations. Pollution, invasive species, and human disturbances further stress urban ecosystems. Climate change intensifies these pressures by increasing heat stress, altering rainfall patterns, and introducing new pests and diseases. Inequities in access to green spaces exacerbate social and environmental injustices, with marginalized communities often having fewer opportunities to benefit from urban biodiversity. Addressing these challenges requires coordinated planning, management, and community engagement.

Efforts to enhance urban biodiversity and habitats include the creation and restoration of green infrastructure, such as green roofs, vertical gardens, and urban forests. Cities are increasingly adopting nature-based solutions that integrate ecological functions into planning and design. Wildlife-friendly urban planning, including the preservation of corridors and the reduction of barriers such as roads and fences, supports species movement and connectivity. Policy instruments, community initiatives, and citizen science projects also play vital roles in monitoring and protecting urban biodiversity. These strategies align ecological conservation with urban development, creating multifunctional landscapes that benefit both people and nature.

Urban biodiversity and habitats exemplify how natural capital can be conserved and enhanced even in human-dominated landscapes. By providing regulating, provisioning, supporting, and cultural services, they contribute to ecological resilience, public health, and cultural vitality. Recognizing the value of biodiversity within cities and embedding it into planning and governance ensures that urban environments remain livable, sustainable, and resilient in a rapidly urbanizing world.

Public Health and Well-Being Benefits

The relationship between natural capital and public health is profound, with ecosystems and biodiversity directly and indirectly supporting human well-being. Natural environments provide clean air, safe water, nutritious food, and medicines, while also offering cultural and psychological benefits that contribute to quality of life. Recognizing the public health and well-being benefits of natural capital underscores its role as a foundation not only for ecological and economic systems but also for human survival and flourishing.

One of the most direct ways natural capital supports health is through the provision of clean air and water. Forests, wetlands, and urban green spaces filter pollutants, absorb carbon dioxide, and release oxygen, improving air quality and reducing the risks of respiratory and cardiovascular diseases. Freshwater ecosystems regulate water flows and filter contaminants, ensuring safe supplies for drinking, hygiene, and sanitation. These services are critical for reducing the global burden of disease, particularly in rapidly urbanizing areas where pollution poses significant health risks. Without these ecological services, public health systems would face enormous costs in treating preventable conditions and providing artificial substitutes.

Food security and nutrition are also closely tied to natural capital. Agricultural landscapes, fisheries, and biodiversity provide the raw materials for diets that sustain billions of people. Diverse ecosystems support pollination, soil fertility, and genetic resources that underpin agricultural productivity. Fish and aquatic systems contribute vital proteins and micronutrients, while forests supply fruits, nuts, and medicinal plants. Access to diverse and nutritious food is essential for preventing malnutrition and related health problems, making natural capital a cornerstone of global health. Degraded ecosystems threaten not only food availability but also dietary quality, with direct consequences for public health.

Medicinal resources derived from biodiversity illustrate another important health benefit of natural capital. Plants, fungi, and marine organisms have long provided the basis for traditional medicines and modern pharmaceuticals. Many widely used drugs, including treatments for cancer, pain, and infections, originate from natural compounds. Ecosystems thus act as vast pharmacies, offering genetic and biochemical resources with untapped potential for future medical discoveries. Protecting biodiversity ensures that these resources remain available for developing new therapies and addressing emerging health challenges.

Beyond physical health, natural capital plays a critical role in psychological and social well-being. Access to green and blue spaces is associated with reduced stress, improved mood, and better cognitive functioning. Time spent in natural environments can lower blood pressure, reduce anxiety, and enhance mental resilience. Urban parks, forests, rivers, and coastlines provide opportunities for recreation and exercise, contributing to physical fitness and lowering risks of obesity, diabetes, and other chronic diseases. These cultural services highlight the non-material but highly significant contributions of natural capital to human well-being.

Social equity and community health are also influenced by access to natural capital. Communities with abundant green spaces often experience better health outcomes, while marginalized populations with limited access face disproportionate health risks. Unequal distribution of natural resources can exacerbate health disparities, particularly in urban areas where low-income neighborhoods may lack safe, accessible parks or clean water. Ensuring equitable access to natural capital is therefore not only an environmental issue but also a public health imperative. Policies that integrate green infrastructure and promote inclusive urban design can reduce health inequalities and improve overall community well-being.

Natural capital also reduces health risks by mitigating hazards. Wetlands and coastal systems buffer against floods and storms, protecting human settlements and reducing injury and disease outbreaks. Forests regulate local climates, reducing the intensity of heat waves that can cause heat-related illnesses and deaths. By stabilizing ecosystems and reducing exposure to hazards, natural capital functions as a form of preventive healthcare, lowering the need for costly emergency responses. This protective role will become increasingly important as climate change intensifies risks to health and safety.

Challenges remain in fully realizing the health benefits of natural capital. Rapid urbanization, industrialization, and ecosystem degradation threaten the quality and availability of natural resources. Pollution, deforestation, and overextraction undermine the ability of ecosystems to deliver clean air, water, and food. Climate change compounds these pressures, altering disease patterns, intensifying disasters, and destabilizing food and water supplies. Addressing these challenges requires integrating public health goals into environmental policies and recognizing the interdependence of ecosystems and human well-being.

Public health and well-being benefits highlight the essential role of natural capital in sustaining life and enhancing quality of life. By providing clean air and water, nutritious food, medicinal resources, psychological support, and protection from hazards, ecosystems form the foundation of human health. Safeguarding and restoring natural capital is therefore not only an ecological or economic priority but also a critical investment in global health and well-being.

Governance of Urban Natural Capital

Governance of urban natural capital involves the systems, policies, and institutions that guide how cities conserve, manage, and integrate natural assets into development strategies. As urban areas expand, governance becomes essential to balance competing demands for land, resources, and infrastructure while ensuring that ecosystems continue to provide vital services. Effective governance frameworks recognize the ecological, economic, and social values of urban natural capital and embed them in planning, decision-making, and community engagement.

At the core of governance are municipal authorities, which play a central role in managing green spaces, water resources, and biodiversity within city boundaries. Local governments establish zoning regulations, land-use plans, and development guidelines that determine how urban land is allocated and managed. Their decisions influence the extent and quality of parks, urban forests, wetlands, and river corridors. Effective municipal governance requires integrating ecological considerations into core urban planning functions, ensuring that natural capital is not treated as an afterthought but as a foundation of urban sustainability.

National and regional governments also shape the governance of urban natural capital by providing policy frameworks, funding, and regulatory oversight. National biodiversity strategies, climate action plans, and urban development policies often include guidelines for protecting and enhancing ecosystems within cities. Regional authorities may coordinate across municipalities to manage shared natural resources such as watersheds or coastal zones. These higher-level frameworks ensure coherence between local initiatives and broader sustainability objectives, while also addressing cross-boundary issues that transcend individual cities.

Institutions responsible for infrastructure and utilities further influence urban natural capital. Water utilities, for example, manage supply systems that depend on watershed protection, while transportation authorities oversee networks that intersect with green corridors. Decisions about infrastructure design and maintenance can either degrade or enhance ecosystems. Increasingly, governance frameworks encourage infrastructure agencies to adopt nature-based solutions, such as green roofs, bioswales, or restored wetlands, that deliver both service reliability and ecological benefits.

The private sector is another critical actor in governance. Developers, businesses, and investors make decisions that shape urban landscapes through construction projects, supply chains, and financial flows. Corporate strategies that account for natural capital can reduce ecological impacts and enhance sustainability. Incentives such as green building certifications, tax benefits for conservation, and sustainability-linked finance mechanisms encourage businesses to align with ecological objectives. Governance frameworks that engage the private sector expand the capacity for investment in urban natural capital while fostering innovation in sustainable design and management.

Civil society and community organizations contribute significantly to governance by advocating for environmental protection, participating in planning processes, and managing local projects. NGOs, neighborhood associations, and citizen groups often drive initiatives to create community gardens, restore wetlands, or monitor urban biodiversity. Their involvement strengthens accountability, ensures that governance reflects local priorities, and builds public support for ecological initiatives. Empowering communities to participate in governance enhances inclusivity and legitimacy, while tapping into local knowledge and stewardship.

Effective governance of urban natural capital requires coordination across these diverse actors. Fragmentation of responsibilities between government departments, agencies, and stakeholders can undermine effectiveness. Integrated governance models emphasize cross-sectoral collaboration, data sharing, and joint decision-making. Mechanisms such as urban environmental councils, multi-stakeholder platforms, and participatory planning processes facilitate dialogue and align efforts across institutions. Coordinated governance ensures that policies addressing housing, transportation, energy, and green space are coherent and mutually reinforcing.

Challenges to governance remain significant. Limited financial resources, political constraints, and competing development priorities often hinder the protection of natural capital in cities. Rapid urbanization can place pressure on ecosystems, while weak enforcement of regulations allows degradation to continue. Inequalities in access to green spaces highlight the need for governance approaches that prioritize equity and justice, ensuring that all residents benefit from urban ecosystems. Addressing these challenges requires strong institutions, transparent decision-making, and innovative financing mechanisms that secure long-term investment in urban natural capital.

Governance of urban natural capital is ultimately about integrating ecological values into the fabric of urban life. By aligning municipal planning, national policies, private sector actions, and community engagement, governance systems can ensure that cities remain resilient, inclusive, and sustainable. Strengthening these governance frameworks is essential for enabling natural capital to continue delivering the services that underpin human well-being and urban prosperity.

Chapter 8: Natural Capital in Climate Mitigation and Adaptation

Natural capital plays a vital role in both mitigating climate change and enabling adaptation to its impacts. Ecosystems regulate greenhouse gases by sequestering and storing carbon, while also buffering communities against floods, droughts, storms, and heat waves. Forests, wetlands, soils, and oceans function as natural infrastructures that provide long-term, cost-effective solutions to global climate challenges.

This chapter explores how natural capital contributes to reducing emissions, enhancing resilience, and supporting adaptation strategies across scales. It emphasizes the importance of integrating ecosystem-based approaches into climate policy, ensuring that mitigation and adaptation efforts align with biodiversity protection and sustainable development.

Carbon Sequestration and Storage

Carbon sequestration and storage are essential processes through which natural capital contributes to climate regulation and the stability of Earth's systems. They involve the capture of carbon dioxide from the atmosphere and its storage in vegetation, soils, oceans, and geological formations. By absorbing and storing carbon, ecosystems mitigate the effects of anthropogenic greenhouse gas emissions, reducing the pace of climate change. Recognizing carbon sequestration and storage as ecosystem services highlights the critical role of natural capital in sustaining planetary health and human well-being.

Forests are among the most significant terrestrial systems for carbon sequestration. Trees absorb carbon dioxide during photosynthesis, storing it in their biomass and transferring it to soils through roots and organic matter. Tropical rainforests, boreal forests, and mangroves are especially effective in sequestering carbon due to their size, density, and productivity. Forest soils continue to store carbon for long periods, creating a durable reservoir. Sustainable forest management, reforestation, and afforestation enhance these processes, while deforestation and degradation release stored carbon back into the atmosphere, undermining climate goals.

Grasslands and drylands also contribute substantially to carbon storage, particularly in their soils. Unlike forests, where most carbon is stored in biomass, grasslands store the majority of carbon underground. This makes them resilient to disturbances such as fires, which may burn vegetation but leave soil carbon largely intact. Practices such as rotational grazing, cover cropping, and restoration of degraded rangelands enhance the capacity of these ecosystems to sequester and retain carbon. Protecting grasslands from conversion to croplands is critical, as plowing releases significant amounts of soil carbon.

Wetlands, peatlands, and coastal ecosystems are particularly important carbon sinks, often referred to as "blue carbon" systems. Peatlands store enormous amounts of carbon in waterlogged soils, where slow decomposition allows organic matter to accumulate over millennia. Coastal ecosystems such as mangroves, salt marshes, and seagrass meadows sequester carbon at exceptionally high rates, both in vegetation and in sediments. Despite occupying relatively small areas, these ecosystems store disproportionate amounts of carbon. Their conservation and restoration are vital strategies for climate mitigation, as their degradation releases large quantities of greenhouse gases.

Oceans play a central role in global carbon sequestration, absorbing a significant portion of anthropogenic carbon dioxide emissions. Phytoplankton in surface waters capture carbon through photosynthesis, forming the base of marine food webs. Some of this carbon sinks to deeper layers, where it can remain sequestered for centuries. Marine ecosystems such as kelp forests and coral reefs also contribute to carbon storage. However, rising carbon dioxide levels are causing ocean acidification, threatening biodiversity and altering the capacity of marine systems to store carbon effectively.

Maintaining healthy oceans is therefore essential for sustaining their role in carbon sequestration.

Soil systems across ecosystems represent another critical component of carbon storage. Organic matter derived from plant litter, root exudates, and microbial activity accumulates in soils, where it can be stabilized by physical and chemical processes. Soils store more carbon globally than the atmosphere and vegetation combined, underscoring their importance as natural capital. Agricultural practices have a major influence on soil carbon levels. Intensive tillage, overuse of chemical inputs, and monocultures deplete soil organic matter, while conservation practices such as agroforestry, no-till farming, and organic amendments enhance soil carbon storage.

Despite their importance, carbon sequestration systems face significant threats. Land-use change, deforestation, overgrazing, and wetland drainage all release stored carbon, reducing the capacity of ecosystems to act as sinks. Climate change itself poses risks, with rising temperatures accelerating decomposition and increasing the frequency of fires, storms, and droughts that destabilize carbon reservoirs. Protecting and enhancing sequestration systems requires integrated management strategies that link conservation, restoration, and sustainable land use.

Carbon sequestration and storage illustrate the role of natural capital in regulating Earth's climate. Forests, grasslands, wetlands, soils, and oceans act as vital sinks, capturing and storing carbon while supporting biodiversity and human well-being. Safeguarding these systems through conservation, restoration, and sustainable practices ensures that natural capital continues to mitigate climate change and sustain ecological and economic resilience.

Climate Resilience and Adaptation Services

Climate resilience and adaptation services provided by natural capital are essential for helping societies cope with the impacts of a changing climate. Ecosystems not only buffer communities against extreme events but also create pathways for long-term adaptation by sustaining resources, regulating environmental processes, and supporting livelihoods. As climate risks intensify, the role of natural systems as providers of resilience and adaptation services becomes increasingly vital for both human and ecological well-being.

One of the primary contributions of natural capital to resilience is its ability to reduce disaster risks. Coastal ecosystems such as mangroves, salt marshes, and coral reefs protect shorelines from storm surges, waves, and erosion. Wetlands absorb excess rainfall, lowering flood peaks and safeguarding downstream settlements. Forests on hillsides stabilize soils and reduce the risks of landslides, while urban green spaces mitigate heat waves by cooling microclimates. These natural defenses often provide more cost-effective and sustainable protection than engineered infrastructure, making them indispensable assets in adaptation strategies.

Natural capital also enhances resilience by maintaining water security under changing climate conditions. Watersheds and forests regulate hydrological cycles, ensuring reliable water supplies even during droughts or periods of variable rainfall. Wetlands recharge aquifers and filter pollutants, securing water quality in times of scarcity. In agricultural systems, practices such as agroforestry and soil conservation enhance resilience by retaining soil moisture and reducing vulnerability to drought. By sustaining the quantity and quality of water resources, ecosystems underpin adaptation in both rural and urban contexts.

Food security is another area where natural capital supports climate resilience. Diverse agricultural landscapes, fisheries, and genetic resources provide the basis for adapting food systems to climate variability. Biodiversity in crops and livestock breeds enhances resilience to pests, diseases, and changing weather patterns. Coastal and inland fisheries supported by healthy aquatic ecosystems contribute protein and nutrients to vulnerable populations. By safeguarding the ecological foundations of food production, natural capital ensures that communities can adapt to disruptions in supply and shifting growing conditions.

Health and well-being benefits derived from natural capital also contribute to climate resilience. Access to green and blue spaces reduces stress, supports mental health, and strengthens community cohesion, which are important for coping with climate-related challenges. Ecosystems reduce exposure to hazards such as heat, floods, and vector-borne diseases, lowering the health burden of climate change. Furthermore, medicinal resources derived from biodiversity expand options for addressing emerging health challenges associated with shifting disease patterns. These services illustrate how ecosystems support resilience by protecting and promoting public health.

Natural capital plays a role in sustaining livelihoods and economic resilience. Rural and coastal communities often depend directly on forests, fisheries, and agricultural systems for income and subsistence. Protecting and restoring these ecosystems enhances their productivity and reduces vulnerability to climate shocks. Urban natural capital, including green infrastructure and biodiversity, supports jobs in landscaping, recreation, and tourism, diversifying income sources. Ecosystem-based adaptation strategies also create opportunities for innovation and investment, aligning economic resilience with environmental stewardship.

Equity and inclusivity are central to the resilience benefits of natural capital. Vulnerable groups, including low-income communities, indigenous peoples, and women, often depend most directly on ecosystems for survival and are disproportionately affected by climate change. Ensuring their access to natural resources, participation in governance, and recognition of traditional knowledge strengthens adaptation strategies. Community-based management of forests, fisheries, and watersheds exemplifies how governance can align ecological resilience with social justice.

Challenges to realizing these benefits include ecosystem degradation, competing land uses, and insufficient recognition of ecosystem services in policy and planning. Unsustainable practices such as deforestation, wetland drainage, and overfishing erode the resilience capacity of ecosystems. Urbanization often replaces natural buffers with impervious surfaces, increasing exposure to hazards. Addressing these challenges requires integrating natural capital into adaptation planning, creating supportive policies, and investing in restoration and conservation.

Climate resilience and adaptation services demonstrate how ecosystems act as allies in addressing climate risks. By reducing hazards, securing resources, sustaining food and health systems, and supporting livelihoods, natural capital provides a foundation for adaptive capacity. Safeguarding and enhancing these services ensures that societies are better equipped to navigate the uncertainties of a changing climate while promoting sustainable development.

Nature-Based Solutions and Climate Policy

Nature-based solutions are approaches that harness ecosystems and natural processes to address societal challenges, particularly those associated with climate change. By protecting, restoring, and sustainably managing ecosystems, nature-based solutions provide multiple benefits: reducing greenhouse gas emissions, enhancing resilience to climate impacts, supporting biodiversity, and delivering economic and social gains. Their integration into climate policy represents a critical step toward achieving sustainability goals while aligning ecological integrity with human development.

One of the primary contributions of nature-based solutions to climate policy is their role in climate mitigation. Forest conservation, reforestation, and afforestation enhance carbon sequestration, while the restoration of peatlands, mangroves, and seagrass meadows locks carbon in soils and sediments. These measures not only reduce atmospheric carbon dioxide but also support biodiversity and water regulation. Compared to technological approaches, nature-based solutions often provide cost-effective and scalable pathways to reducing emissions, making them attractive for national climate strategies and international commitments.

Equally significant is their contribution to climate adaptation. Natural systems buffer communities against climate hazards, reducing vulnerability and supporting resilience. Wetlands and mangroves protect coastlines from storm surges and flooding, urban green spaces mitigate heat stress, and restored watersheds secure water supplies during droughts. These services demonstrate how ecosystems act as natural infrastructure, providing long-term and adaptive benefits that complement or replace engineered solutions. By embedding nature-based solutions into adaptation strategies, policymakers can strengthen resilience while conserving natural capital.

Nature-based solutions also intersect with broader policy objectives, such as sustainable development and biodiversity conservation. Initiatives that restore ecosystems or promote sustainable agriculture often generate co-benefits, from enhancing food security to creating green jobs. They align closely with the Sustainable Development Goals, particularly those addressing climate action, life on land, and life below water. In this sense, nature-based solutions represent a bridge between climate policy, environmental stewardship, and socio-economic development.

The incorporation of nature-based solutions into climate policy is gaining traction at multiple levels. International frameworks, such as the Paris Agreement, recognize the importance of ecosystems in both mitigation and adaptation efforts. Many countries include nature-based measures in their nationally determined contributions, committing to actions such as forest restoration or coastal protection. Regional initiatives also promote collaboration across borders to manage shared resources, while cities are embedding green infrastructure into climate action plans. These policy pathways highlight the growing recognition of ecosystems as allies in climate governance.

Despite their promise, challenges remain in fully integrating nature-based solutions into climate policy. One barrier is the difficulty of quantifying benefits, particularly when ecosystem services are complex, interdependent, and location-specific. Valuation uncertainties can limit investment and policy support. Land-use conflicts also arise, as restoration and conservation initiatives may compete with agricultural, industrial, or urban development. Ensuring equity is another challenge, as projects that prioritize carbon sequestration may inadvertently marginalize local communities or overlook cultural values tied to ecosystems. Overcoming these challenges requires transparent governance, participatory planning, and robust monitoring systems.

Financing is another critical consideration. While the long-term benefits of nature-based solutions are clear, upfront investments can be substantial, and returns may take years to materialize. Mobilizing public and private finance, developing innovative instruments such as green bonds or carbon markets, and aligning subsidies with ecological goals are essential to scaling these solutions. Integrating them into mainstream climate finance frameworks ensures that they receive sustained support alongside technological and infrastructural investments.

Nature-based solutions represent a powerful opportunity for climate policy, combining ecological effectiveness with socio-economic benefits. They mitigate emissions, strengthen adaptation, and contribute to broader sustainability objectives. By embedding them in policies, planning, and financing mechanisms, governments and institutions can ensure that ecosystems remain central to global climate strategies. Their success depends on inclusive governance, adequate investment, and recognition of the diverse values that natural systems provide.

Integrating Climate and Natural Capital Strategies

Integrating climate and natural capital strategies is essential for creating cohesive approaches that address environmental, economic, and social challenges simultaneously. Climate change and natural capital are deeply interconnected: ecosystems act as carbon sinks, regulate water and temperature, and protect against hazards, while their degradation amplifies climate risks. Recognizing these interdependencies allows policymakers, businesses, and communities to design strategies that align mitigation, adaptation, and conservation goals, maximizing co-benefits while reducing trade-offs.

One of the strongest arguments for integration lies in the complementary role of ecosystems in climate mitigation. Forests, wetlands, grasslands, and oceans sequester and store vast amounts of carbon, making them critical natural allies in reducing greenhouse gas concentrations. Conservation and restoration of these systems directly support climate targets while simultaneously preserving biodiversity, water resources, and soil fertility. When climate policies are aligned with natural capital strategies, mitigation efforts expand beyond technological solutions to include ecosystem-based approaches that are cost-effective and multifunctional.

Adaptation is another domain where integrated strategies yield significant benefits. Natural capital provides adaptation services by reducing vulnerability to climate hazards and enhancing resilience. Coastal ecosystems such as mangroves and salt marshes protect communities from storm surges, wetlands absorb floodwaters, and urban green spaces mitigate heat stress. These services complement engineered infrastructure, often at lower costs and with broader ecological and social benefits. Integrating adaptation strategies with natural capital management ensures that climate resilience is built on a foundation of healthy ecosystems capable of sustaining long-term protection.

Economic and financial systems also benefit from integrated strategies. Natural capital accounting provides a framework for measuring the contributions of ecosystems to economic stability, enabling climate-related investments to capture the full value of ecological services. For instance, incorporating natural capital into cost-benefit analyses of climate projects ensures that ecosystem services such as water regulation or carbon storage are recognized alongside financial returns. Green bonds, sustainability-linked finance, and carbon markets can be structured to fund initiatives that advance both climate goals and ecosystem conservation. This alignment strengthens the financial case for investments that deliver ecological and climate resilience simultaneously.

Policy frameworks increasingly recognize the value of integration. Many countries have incorporated ecosystem-based approaches into their nationally determined contributions under the Paris Agreement, linking climate action with natural capital management. National adaptation plans often include strategies for protecting forests, wetlands, and watersheds as part of climate resilience. At the regional level, cross-border initiatives for river basin management or coastal protection demonstrate how shared ecosystems can serve as platforms for integrated climate and natural capital governance. Embedding these linkages into policies ensures coherence across sectors, reducing duplication and enhancing effectiveness.

Integration also strengthens equity and inclusivity in climate and environmental governance. Communities most vulnerable to climate change often rely heavily on natural capital for their livelihoods, from smallholder farmers and fishers to indigenous peoples. By linking climate policies with natural capital strategies, governance systems can prioritize the needs of these groups, ensuring access to resources, participation in decision-making, and recognition of traditional knowledge. This inclusivity not only enhances social justice but also improves the effectiveness of climate and conservation initiatives by drawing on local expertise and stewardship.

However, integration faces several challenges. Institutional silos remain a barrier, with climate and environmental governance often managed by separate agencies or departments. Differences in funding streams, methodologies, and priorities can create fragmentation, reducing coherence and efficiency. Technical challenges also arise in measuring and valuing ecosystem services within climate frameworks, particularly when benefits are complex or location-specific. Overcoming these challenges requires institutional reforms, cross-sector collaboration, and investment in data, monitoring, and capacity-building.

Private sector engagement is critical to advancing integrated strategies. Businesses increasingly recognize that climate risks are linked to natural capital dependencies, such as water availability, soil fertility, and biodiversity. Incorporating natural capital into corporate climate strategies enables companies to anticipate risks, reduce impacts, and create new opportunities for innovation. Supply chain management, product design, and investment portfolios can all be aligned with integrated approaches that enhance both climate performance and ecological sustainability. Transparent reporting frameworks further ensure accountability and build investor confidence.

Integrating climate and natural capital strategies provides a pathway toward holistic sustainability. By aligning ecosystem management with mitigation and adaptation efforts, societies can leverage synergies that enhance resilience, protect biodiversity, and support equitable development. Success depends on strong governance, inclusive participation, innovative financing, and the recognition that ecosystems and climate are inseparable dimensions of the same challenge. This integrated approach ensures that environmental strategies are not only more effective but also more equitable and enduring.

Chapter 9: Future Directions for Natural Capital

The future of natural capital lies in deepening its integration into economic systems, governance frameworks, and societal values. As pressures on ecosystems intensify, the challenge is to move beyond recognition of natural capital's importance toward transformative action that secures its role in sustaining life and prosperity. Emerging technologies, innovative financial instruments, and evolving governance models offer pathways for scaling up conservation, restoration, and sustainable use.

This chapter considers future directions for natural capital, examining opportunities to strengthen science-policy interfaces, embed ecological values into finance, embrace inclusivity and equity, and align natural capital strategies with global sustainability and climate goals.

Emerging Theories and Concepts

The field of natural capital has evolved rapidly, giving rise to emerging theories and concepts that expand its scope and deepen its application across science, policy, and practice. These ideas reflect growing recognition of the interconnectedness of ecological systems, human well-being, and economic prosperity, while also responding to the limitations of earlier frameworks. By exploring new perspectives, researchers and practitioners are shaping a more comprehensive and adaptive understanding of natural capital in the 21st century.

One emerging concept is the idea of planetary boundaries. This framework identifies critical ecological thresholds that regulate the stability of Earth systems, such as climate change, biodiversity loss, freshwater use, and land system change. Crossing these boundaries risks destabilizing the conditions that have allowed human societies to flourish. Linking natural capital with planetary boundaries emphasizes the finite nature of ecological systems and highlights the importance of maintaining global environmental integrity. It reframes natural capital not just as an asset but as the foundation of a safe operating space for humanity.

Another important development is the concept of ecosystem-based approaches, which apply ecological principles to address multiple societal challenges simultaneously. Ecosystem-based adaptation, for example, uses ecosystems to reduce vulnerability to climate impacts, while ecosystem-based mitigation focuses on enhancing carbon sequestration and storage. These approaches bridge natural capital theory with practical strategies, integrating biodiversity conservation, climate resilience, and sustainable development. They highlight the multifunctionality of ecosystems and the synergies that can be realized when policies and investments prioritize natural processes.

The integration of social and cultural values into natural capital theory is also gaining attention. Traditional frameworks often emphasized economic valuation, sometimes overlooking the intrinsic, cultural, and spiritual dimensions of ecosystems. Emerging concepts such as relational values recognize that people's connections to nature are not solely utilitarian but also rooted in identity, heritage, and community. This perspective broadens the understanding of natural capital, making it more inclusive and reflective of diverse worldviews. It also underscores the need for governance systems that respect and incorporate indigenous knowledge and practices.

Digital and technological innovations are driving new theories about how to measure and manage natural capital. Advances in remote sensing, artificial intelligence, and big data analytics allow for real-time monitoring of ecosystems, improving accuracy and scalability. Concepts such as digital twins of ecosystems—virtual models that simulate ecological processes—are being developed to forecast changes and inform decision-making. These tools enhance transparency and accountability, bridging gaps between science, policy, and business while making natural capital assessments more dynamic and predictive.

The idea of natural capital as a form of infrastructure is another emerging concept. Known as natural infrastructure, this framework positions ecosystems alongside built infrastructure in planning and investment. Wetlands, forests, and reefs are recognized as providing services equivalent to dams, levees, or water treatment plants, often at lower costs and with co-benefits such as biodiversity conservation. Viewing ecosystems as infrastructure challenges conventional development paradigms and creates opportunities for integrating natural capital into mainstream economic and urban planning.

In the financial sector, new concepts such as nature-related financial risk are transforming how natural capital is framed. Recognizing that ecosystem degradation poses systemic risks to economies, financial institutions are beginning to account for dependencies on natural systems within portfolios and investment strategies. Initiatives like the Task Force on Nature-related Financial Disclosures reflect this shift, highlighting the importance of transparency and accountability in managing nature-related risks. This evolution aligns natural capital with global financial governance, creating pathways for large-scale mobilization of capital toward conservation and restoration.

Ethical considerations are also shaping emerging theories. Debates about rights of nature challenge the framing of ecosystems purely as capital, instead emphasizing legal personhood for rivers, forests, and other natural entities. This concept reorients governance toward stewardship and justice, recognizing ecosystems as subjects with inherent rights rather than objects of exploitation. While controversial, such approaches are influencing policy and legal frameworks in countries where natural systems have been granted legal status, expanding the theoretical boundaries of natural capital.

These emerging theories and concepts illustrate the dynamism of natural capital as a field. They integrate ecological science with social, cultural, financial, and technological perspectives, creating a multidimensional understanding of ecosystems as essential foundations of human and planetary well-being. By expanding beyond narrow economic valuation and embracing inclusivity, resilience, and justice, these developments ensure that natural capital theory remains relevant, adaptable, and transformative in addressing global environmental challenges.

Digital Tools and Data Innovations

Digital tools and data innovations are transforming how natural capital is measured, monitored, and managed. Advances in technology allow for unprecedented levels of precision and scale in tracking ecosystem functions, valuing services, and integrating ecological data into decision-making processes. By making natural capital more visible and quantifiable, digital innovations help bridge the gap between ecological science, policy, and finance, ensuring that natural assets are recognized as critical components of sustainable development.

Remote sensing technologies represent one of the most important innovations in monitoring natural capital. Satellites equipped with high-resolution sensors provide continuous data on land cover, vegetation health, water quality, and atmospheric conditions. These tools make it possible to track deforestation, urban expansion, wetland loss, and agricultural practices across the globe in real time. Emerging platforms combine satellite data with machine learning to detect changes more quickly and accurately, enabling policymakers, businesses, and communities to respond proactively to ecosystem degradation.

GIS expand the utility of remote sensing by allowing data to be analyzed and visualized spatially. GIS platforms integrate multiple data sources to create maps and models that highlight patterns and trends in natural capital. For example, watershed health, biodiversity hotspots, or carbon storage capacity can be mapped at local, regional, or global scales. These visualizations make complex ecological data accessible to decision-makers, supporting land-use planning, conservation prioritization, and environmental risk assessments.

The rise of big data and cloud-based platforms has also revolutionized natural capital management. Large volumes of ecological, climatic, and socio-economic data can now be processed and stored efficiently, enabling comprehensive analyses of ecosystem services. Cloud computing platforms facilitate collaboration across organizations and geographies, ensuring that datasets are updated and accessible in real time. This has improved transparency, accountability, and inclusivity in how natural capital information is used in governance and business.

Artificial intelligence (AI) and machine learning are increasingly applied to ecological datasets, uncovering patterns that would be difficult to detect through conventional methods. AI models can predict land-use change, estimate ecosystem service values, and simulate the effects of policy interventions on natural capital. By analyzing vast datasets, machine learning algorithms enhance the ability to forecast risks and opportunities, providing decision-makers with actionable insights. These tools are particularly valuable in contexts where time-sensitive responses are needed, such as monitoring illegal logging or predicting drought impacts.

Citizen science and digital participation platforms represent another innovation, empowering communities to contribute to natural capital monitoring. Mobile applications allow individuals to record biodiversity sightings, water quality observations, or land-use changes, feeding data into larger databases. These contributions expand the coverage of monitoring systems and promote public engagement with ecological stewardship. At the same time, digital participation platforms enable stakeholders to share information and co-create solutions, enhancing the inclusivity and legitimacy of natural capital governance.

Blockchain and distributed ledger technologies offer potential for creating transparent and verifiable systems of natural capital accounting. These tools can track the provenance of ecosystem services, such as carbon credits or sustainably harvested products, ensuring credibility and reducing risks of fraud. Smart contracts embedded in blockchain systems can automate payments for ecosystem services, creating efficient and accountable markets that link conservation with economic incentives. By enhancing trust, these technologies support scaling up finance for natural capital protection and restoration.

Digital innovations are also driving the creation of natural capital dashboards and indices that integrate multiple data streams into comprehensive indicators. These platforms provide policymakers and businesses with clear overviews of ecosystem health, service flows, and economic dependencies. Dashboards can track progress toward sustainability targets, identify risks from ecosystem degradation, and highlight investment opportunities. By making ecological data more tangible, they help align governance, finance, and conservation efforts with the realities of natural capital.

Despite their promise, digital tools face challenges related to data gaps, accessibility, and equity. Many regions, particularly in the Global South, lack the infrastructure or capacity to fully leverage advanced technologies. Data privacy and ownership issues also raise concerns about who controls and benefits from digital information on ecosystems. Addressing these challenges requires building capacity, fostering open data initiatives, and ensuring that digital innovations are inclusive and equitable.

Digital tools and data innovations represent a transformative frontier for natural capital management. By enhancing measurement, monitoring, and integration, they make the invisible visible, bringing ecosystems into the center of decision-making. From remote sensing and AI to blockchain and participatory platforms, these technologies are enabling new forms of transparency, accountability, and collaboration, strengthening the recognition of natural capital as a foundation for sustainable futures.

Cross-Sectoral Integration Pathways

Cross-sectoral integration pathways are essential for aligning policies, practices, and investments that affect natural capital across diverse areas such as energy, agriculture, water, health, and urban development. Because ecosystems provide services that cut across boundaries, siloed approaches often fail to capture the full value of natural capital or address the complex challenges of sustainability. Integrating across sectors creates synergies, reduces trade-offs, and ensures that natural capital considerations are embedded in decision-making at multiple levels.

One of the most important integration pathways lies between agriculture and water management. Agricultural systems depend heavily on freshwater for irrigation, livestock, and processing, while watersheds and aquifers rely on sustainable land-use practices to maintain flow and quality. Practices such as integrated watershed management, efficient irrigation, and soil conservation support both food security and water resilience. By linking agricultural and water policies, governments can ensure that farming practices sustain water resources while water governance systems safeguard the ecological foundations of food production.

Energy systems provide another critical area for integration. Fossil fuel extraction and energy infrastructure often degrade ecosystems, while renewable energy development requires careful land-use planning to avoid biodiversity loss. At the same time, ecosystems such as forests and wetlands play vital roles in regulating energy systems by sequestering carbon and stabilizing local climates. Cross-sectoral pathways that integrate natural capital into energy policy can prioritize renewable energy solutions with low ecological footprints, invest in ecosystem restoration to offset emissions, and design infrastructure that coexists with natural systems.

The intersection of health and natural capital highlights another pathway. Ecosystems provide clean air, safe water, nutritious food, and recreational spaces that directly support physical and mental health. Yet health systems often address outcomes without considering environmental determinants. Integrating natural capital into health policy ensures that prevention, resilience, and well-being are prioritized through investments in green infrastructure, pollution control, and ecosystem restoration. This reduces health care costs while improving quality of life, particularly for vulnerable populations most exposed to environmental risks.

Urban development presents further opportunities for integration. Cities often expand at the expense of natural ecosystems, yet urban sustainability depends on access to clean water, air, and green spaces. Cross-sectoral pathways link urban planning with ecosystem management by embedding green infrastructure, conserving biodiversity, and designing climate-resilient landscapes. For example, integrating transport, housing, and energy policies with ecological considerations reduces pollution, enhances livability, and strengthens resilience. These approaches not only safeguard natural capital but also improve equity by ensuring that benefits are accessible to all urban residents.

Cross-sectoral integration is also vital for aligning climate policy with natural capital strategies. Climate mitigation and adaptation depend heavily on ecosystem services such as carbon sequestration, water regulation, and disaster risk reduction. When climate and biodiversity policies are designed separately, opportunities for synergy are lost, and conflicts may emerge, such as afforestation projects that reduce biodiversity. Pathways that align climate and natural capital strategies ensure that mitigation and adaptation measures strengthen ecosystems while ecosystems themselves enhance climate resilience.

Institutional coordination is central to effective integration. Many countries face fragmentation, with ministries of environment, agriculture, energy, and health operating independently. Establishing cross-sectoral councils, inter-ministerial committees, or integrated policy frameworks can reduce duplication and promote coherence. Regional and local governments play an important role by adapting integration strategies to local contexts, while global frameworks such as the Sustainable Development Goals provide overarching guidance. Collaboration between governments, businesses, and civil society further ensures that integration is practical, inclusive, and responsive to diverse needs.

Financing mechanisms are another key pathway. Public budgets, private investments, and international funds are often allocated according to sectoral priorities, which can create competition rather than collaboration. Innovative financing instruments such as blended finance, green bonds, and payments for ecosystem services provide opportunities to fund projects that deliver multiple benefits across sectors. For example, watershed protection initiatives can be financed jointly by water utilities, agricultural producers, and energy companies, reflecting shared dependencies on natural capital.

Challenges to integration include institutional inertia, competing interests, and mismatched time horizons. Sectoral agencies may be reluctant to cede authority, while short-term economic goals often overshadow long-term sustainability objectives. Data gaps and methodological differences further complicate integration, as sectors may use different metrics and valuation systems. Overcoming these barriers requires political leadership, robust data systems, and participatory governance that builds trust and fosters collaboration.

Cross-sectoral integration pathways create opportunities for innovation, efficiency, and resilience. By connecting agriculture, water, energy, health, and urban development, societies can optimize the use of natural capital while addressing complex challenges such as climate change, food security, and public health. These pathways reflect the reality that ecosystems underpin every sector of the economy and that sustainable futures depend on governance systems capable of bridging boundaries. Through collaboration, coordination, and innovation, cross-sectoral integration ensures that natural capital remains a central pillar of sustainable development.

The Road Ahead

The road ahead for natural capital lies in advancing frameworks, policies, and practices that firmly embed ecosystems into the heart of decision-making. As awareness grows about the dependence of economies, societies, and climate stability on functioning ecosystems, momentum is building to elevate natural capital from a peripheral concept to a mainstream driver of sustainability. The challenge and opportunity of the coming decades will be to move from recognition to implementation, ensuring that natural capital is valued, conserved, and restored at scales commensurate with global challenges.

A critical priority is strengthening the scientific foundations of natural capital. Continued innovation in ecological research, remote sensing, and data integration will expand the ability to measure and monitor ecosystem services. Enhanced metrics and valuation methods will provide decision-makers with reliable information on the contributions of natural capital to economic and social systems. Advancing open data platforms and cross-border collaborations will ensure that scientific progress informs governance at local, national, and global levels. Building strong science-policy interfaces will be essential for ensuring that evidence drives effective action.

Another key direction is embedding natural capital into financial systems. Capital markets, banks, and investment institutions increasingly recognize that environmental degradation creates systemic risks. Integrating natural capital into risk assessments, disclosure requirements, and portfolio management will strengthen resilience and unlock new opportunities for sustainable finance. Green bonds, biodiversity credits, and sustainability-linked loans are early examples of how finance can mobilize resources for conservation and restoration. Scaling these instruments requires supportive regulation, credible monitoring, and partnerships between public and private actors. As financial flows align with ecological priorities, natural capital will become a cornerstone of resilient and responsible investment.

Governance systems will also need to evolve. Current institutional arrangements are often fragmented, with responsibilities for natural capital scattered across sectors and agencies. The road ahead requires more integrated and coherent governance, supported by legal frameworks that recognize the value of ecosystems. International agreements, national policies, and local initiatives must work in synergy, guided by shared principles of equity, transparency, and accountability. Inclusive governance that recognizes the rights of communities and indigenous peoples will be essential for ensuring that natural capital strategies are both just and effective.

Technology and innovation will play a transformative role in the future of natural capital. Digital platforms, artificial intelligence, and blockchain offer tools for real-time monitoring, transparent reporting, and efficient markets for ecosystem services. Virtual modeling and predictive analytics will support scenario planning and policy design. These tools, if equitably deployed, can democratize access to information and empower diverse stakeholders to participate in managing natural capital. The challenge will be to ensure that innovation complements ecological stewardship rather than reinforcing extractive approaches.

Restoration of ecosystems will become an increasingly urgent priority. While conservation remains critical, the scale of past degradation necessitates ambitious restoration efforts in forests, wetlands, grasslands, and marine environments. Global initiatives such as the UN Decade on Ecosystem Restoration highlight the importance of mobilizing resources and political will for large-scale efforts. Restoration not only replenishes natural capital but also creates jobs, enhances food and water security, and builds resilience against climate impacts. Scaling these efforts will require clear targets, sustained investment, and strong community involvement.

The road ahead must also address the equity dimensions of natural capital. Benefits from ecosystems are not evenly distributed, and vulnerable groups often bear the costs of degradation. Ensuring fair access to resources, equitable sharing of benefits, and protection of cultural values tied to ecosystems will be central to just transitions. Policies must prioritize inclusivity, respecting diverse worldviews and recognizing the intrinsic as well as instrumental values of natural capital. By addressing inequities, strategies can build legitimacy, strengthen cooperation, and deliver outcomes that benefit both people and nature.

Education and capacity-building will be vital for sustaining progress. Raising awareness of natural capital across schools, universities, businesses, and communities fosters a culture of stewardship. Training programs for policymakers, financial actors, and practitioners ensure that knowledge is translated into action. Investing in education not only builds technical capacity but also nurtures values of responsibility and care for ecosystems. This long-term investment in human capital complements efforts to safeguard natural capital.

The road ahead for natural capital is both challenging and promising. The urgency of biodiversity loss, climate change, and resource pressures demands decisive action. Yet growing recognition of natural capital's importance, coupled with advances in science, finance, technology, and governance, provides a strong foundation for progress. By aligning conservation, restoration, and sustainable use with economic and social systems, societies can secure the benefits of ecosystems for present and future generations. The task now is to act boldly, ensuring that natural capital is not only protected but also placed at the center of sustainable development.

Conclusion

Natural capital has emerged as a central concept for rethinking the relationship between human societies and the ecosystems that sustain them. It reframes the environment not as an external backdrop but as a foundational asset that underpins economies, health, and resilience. Throughout this exploration, natural capital has been shown to extend across forests, grasslands, wetlands, oceans, and urban systems, providing services that regulate climate, secure water, support food systems, and enhance human well-being. Recognizing these contributions is essential for building strategies that ensure sustainability in an era of ecological and climatic uncertainty.

A major theme is the need for stronger integration of natural capital into governance and policy frameworks. Current systems often operate in silos, with environmental, economic, and social policies treated separately. Bridging these divides through coordinated governance ensures that ecosystems are fully accounted for in development planning and climate strategies. International agreements, national frameworks, and local initiatives all play roles in embedding natural capital into decision-making. Equity and inclusivity are equally important, as the benefits of ecosystems are unevenly distributed, and vulnerable communities frequently bear the greatest risks of degradation. Ensuring fair access to resources and incorporating diverse knowledge systems enriches governance and strengthens outcomes.

Finance and markets also form a critical pathway for advancing natural capital. Investment flows, corporate disclosures, and risk assessments are increasingly incorporating ecological considerations, reflecting the reality that ecosystem decline creates systemic risks. Tools such as green bonds, biodiversity credits, and payments for ecosystem services are already creating financial incentives for conservation and restoration. Expanding these mechanisms will align capital with sustainability goals, making natural capital an integral part of economic systems rather than an externality.

Innovation and technology are reshaping how natural capital is understood and managed. Remote sensing, artificial intelligence, and digital platforms provide unprecedented capacity to monitor ecosystems and track their services in real time. These tools support transparency, accountability, and collaboration, while enabling predictive planning in the face of climate change and other pressures. If deployed inclusively, they democratize access to data and empower communities, businesses, and policymakers to make informed choices.

Restoration, alongside conservation, has become an urgent imperative. The scale of ecological degradation requires ambitious efforts to restore forests, wetlands, grasslands, and marine systems. Restoration enhances biodiversity, bolsters carbon storage, and strengthens resilience against climate extremes, offering co-benefits that extend beyond ecology to food security, livelihoods, and public health. Mobilizing resources and political will for large-scale restoration will be essential in the years ahead.

The future of natural capital lies in weaving its principles into the fabric of human systems. Education and capacity-building ensure that individuals and institutions understand its importance and develop the skills to act. Governance and finance must reinforce stewardship, while technology expands the capacity to measure and respond. By bringing together science, policy, business, and society, natural capital can be positioned as the foundation of strategies that secure prosperity within planetary limits.

The task is not only to conserve what remains but also to restore and enhance natural systems so they can continue sustaining life. Natural capital, when fully recognized and integrated, provides a pathway toward resilience, equity, and sustainability. The choices made today will determine whether ecosystems remain capable of supporting future generations, making the stewardship of natural capital one of the defining challenges and opportunities of the century.